Jesus – the Man for others

Copyright 2018 Rodney Schofield

All rights reserved. No part of this publication may be reproduced, stored in a retrieval system, or transmitted in any from or by any means, electronic, mechanical, photocopying, recording or otherwise without prior permission from the publishers.

Published by
Luviri Press
P/Bag 201 Luwinga
Mzuzu 2
Malawi

ISBN 978-99960-60-57-1
eISBN 978-99960-60-58-8

Luviri Press is represented outside Africa by:
African Books Collective Oxford (order@africanbookscollective.com)

www.mzunipress.blogspot.com
www.africanbookscollective.com

editorial assistance and cover: Daniel Neumann

Jesus – the Man for others

Rodney Schofield

Luviri Press
Mzuzu
2018

Contents

1. His vocation	7
The silent years	7
Jesus' public ministry	11
Manifesting his glory	15
2. His social legacy	22
Life in the Spirit	22
An enigmatic future	25
Authentic Christian living	29
3. His mission team	37
The variety of gifts	37
Existing social conventions	38
Complementary roles	41
Later developments	46
4. His cultural embrace	55
Unity and diversity	55
The richness of God's being	61
5. His political challenge	73
The kingdom of God	73
Today's pressing issues	82
6. His message	90
The time is fulfilled	90
Interpreting the language	97

Illustrations

The presentation of Jesus in the Temple	19
Jesus aged 12 disputing with the scribes	20
The baptism of Jesus by John	21
The temptations of Jesus	21
Jesus as the Good Shepherd	34
Jesus casts out a devil	35
Jesus with the Samaritan woman	35
Jesus raises Lazarus from the dead	36
Jesus' entry into Jerusalem	51
Jesus at the Last Supper	52
Jesus before Pilate	53
Jesus crucified	54
Jesus raises Adam and Eve	69
Jesus meets Mary Magdalen in the garden	70
The disciples greet Jesus with their miraculous catch	71
Jesus has ascended	72
The suffering body of Christ	87
Christ's gathered body	87
Christ's missionary outreach	88
The caring body of Christ	89

The cover illustration is taken from an Armenian *khachkar* (cross-stone) at Haghpat c. 1272.
The illustration on page 4 shows a 13th century sculptural relief in the north portal at Chartres Cathedral: it forms part of the creation sequence, and represents Jesus as the Word of God in the act of envisaging humankind.

1. His vocation

The silent years

For most of his life Jesus lived in obscurity:

> When he began his ministry [he] was about thirty years of age, being the son (as was supposed) of Joseph. [Lk 3.23]

There were no doubt good reasons why he had remained quietly in Nazareth until this particular juncture. The last specific mention of Joseph is when Jesus at the age of twelve visited Jerusalem with both his parents for the feast of Passover, as was their custom. It seems clear enough in the gospel records that, once his peripatetic ministry had begun, the only surviving parent was his mother Mary; the presumption is therefore that Joseph had died some time earlier, perhaps when Jesus was a teenager and then took upon himself the role of bread-winner for the household. Caring for his mother was always important to him, hence at the point of his own death he commended Mary into the keeping of 'the disciple whom he loved':

> He said to the disciple, 'Behold, your mother!' And from that hour the disciple took her to his own home. [Jn 19.27]

In Mark's Gospel, generally thought to be the earliest extant record, Jesus is indeed described as 'the carpenter' of Nazareth:

> Is not this the carpenter, the son of Mary and brother of James and Joses and Judas and Simon, and are not his sisters here with us? [Mk 6.3]

Matthew alters this slightly, describing him as 'the carpenter's son', but there is no suggestion even so that the long-serving village carpenter Joseph is still alive. And certainly none of the Gospels give any indication that Jesus had previously stood out as an 'exceptional' figure in his village; the reaction to his teaching is one of 'astonishment', that so ordinary a person could utter such wisdom. The exaggerated stories that appeared in the much later 'infancy gospels' – such as bringing a clay bird to life, or causing a playmate who crossed his path to drop dead – may therefore be ignored.

At what point, we may wonder, did his self-awareness begin to include the uniquely intimate relationship with God that motivated his future ministry? Not many clues are available to us, but Luke's account of his childhood visit to Jerusalem indicates that by the age of twelve he was extremely well-versed in the Hebrew scriptures, more than able to hold his own with learned scribes in the Temple, who were 'amazed' at his understanding. Luke also tells us of his lifetime habit of attending the synagogue each Sabbath day [Lk 4.16], and of his evident literacy. Episodes recorded later indicate that he had thoroughly absorbed the underlying scriptural meanings, interpreting them in very personal terms. On an earlier occasion he speaks of the Temple as 'my Father's house', while eighteen years later in Nazareth he announces himself as the one upon whom Isaiah's prophesied 'Spirit of the Lord' has indeed descended. It is exactly the same when, on the day of his resurrection, he explains recent events to Cleopas and his friend as they walk to Emmaus:

> Beginning with Moses and all the prophets, he interpreted to them in all the scriptures the things *concerning himself.* [Lk 24.27]

In the coming centuries, it was of course the same principle that Christ's followers adopted in their readings of the Old Testament: 'Christ' was the key to its interpretation. Nor was St Jerome speaking out of turn when he commented that 'ignorance of scripture is ignorance of Christ.' It was not, however, the apostles or the early Church Fathers who initiated this insight; it evidently derived from the Lord's own years of quiet reflection on God's word addressed through scripture to himself.

Why though – apart from his family responsibilities – did Jesus begin his public ministry at the particular age of thirty? In Jewish tradition that was usually regarded as the stage in life when a person's full strength was reached – as exemplified in both Joseph and king David:

> Joseph was thirty years old when he entered the service of Pharaoh king of Egypt. [Gen 41.46]

> David was thirty years old when he began to reign. [2 Sam 5.4]

Hence, although the 'legal' age of maturity was variously estimated as eighteen or twenty, *wisdom* was not achieved so readily; a person reckoned as inexperienced might not be too well regarded. By the time

Jesus delivered his message, he was by contrast acclaimed as 'one who had authority, and not as the scribes' [Mk 1.22].

Yet the key to Jesus' emergence from the obscurity of Nazareth at this age actually seems to have been the much publicised preaching of John the Baptist in the Jordan valley. In all four Gospels Jesus' ministry begins with his baptism by John; indeed it actually features in the *opening* verses of Mark's Gospel. The implication seems to be that Jesus saw John's ministry as a divine signal beckoning him into the public arena himself; John was challenging people to turn again to God, in Mark's words taken from Isaiah, as 'one crying in the wilderness: prepare the way of the Lord'. It provided moreover a golden opportunity for Jesus to make his first public gesture: not a statement and certainly not a sermon, but a 'parabolic action' – his humble acceptance of baptism at John's hands. This was his self-identification: the one who came to be among people, whose mission was to share their lot; the one whose readiness to love and serve might enable John's worthy exhortations to be fulfilled. In self-references throughout the Gospels, the language which he generally used was the simple phrase 'the Son of man'. While others sometimes suggested grander (messianic) titles, he himself stressed the humility and humanity of his role.

The accounts of Jesus' baptism are (as with other episodes recorded in the Gospels) not entirely consistent. In John's Gospel, probably the latest to be written, John the Baptist emphasises that 'I myself did not know him'. He also claims to have seen 'the Spirit descend as a dove from heaven' which 'remained on him'. In the other Gospels it appears to have been Jesus himself who experienced this moving spiritual endorsement, and to have been reassured of his own divine Sonship. In the Fourth Gospel there is no mention here of a voice from heaven, but the Baptist expresses a similar testimony in his own words: there appears to be a reference to this later in the Gospel, when Jesus speaking to 'the Jews' notes that they 'sent to John, and he has borne witness to the truth' [Jn 5.33]. However, one should not forget that in the Synoptic Gospels, John the Baptist – now in prison – dispatches messengers to Jesus asking, 'Are you the one who should come, or shall we look for another?' [Mt 11.3 cf. Lk 7.20], which expresses a note of uncertainty in contrast to the ready recognition offered earlier [Mt 3.14]. This is consistent with the growing doubts expressed by others, including disciples of Jesus, that this 'Christ' is not quite the figure they had been expecting.

For his part, Jesus is recorded as paying remarkable tribute to John himself, in words that suggest it may indeed have been his mission centred on the waters of the Jordan that triggered the commencement of Jesus' own ministry:

> Truly, I say to you, among those born of women there has risen no one greater than John the Baptist; yet he who is least in the kingdom of heaven is greater than he. [Mt 11.11 cf. Lk 7.28-30 where the *popular response* to John is emphasized in contrast to his rejection by Jewish authorities.]

If the baptism itself was the very first expression of Jesus' role as 'the Son of man' (a theme to be pursued later), how should the signs from heaven be interpreted? The Spirit 'descending ... like a dove' [Mk 1.10] and the voice from above [Mk 1.11] would seem to be how Jesus felt personally 'affirmed' at that critical stage of his life by his (heavenly) Father. In Luke's version Jesus was actually praying [Lk 3.21] when 'heaven was opened'. His bold move, plunging into the river Jordan in an act of solidarity with God's people, was thereby spiritually endorsed as indeed the right way forward. We can surely only know of the signs – of which he alone was truly aware, in his innermost being – because he later spoke of them to his disciples.

How they subsequently became included in written Gospel records is another matter altogether. The different evangelists no doubt received the oral tradition from more than one source, and made use of it according to the particular circumstances in which they were writing; so – as with most other 'parallel' passages – the descriptive language is varied. With the passage of time, however, the interpretation of this imagery, in which the Spirit is metaphorically 'a dove', plainly got out of hand. What is indicated by it is not any bodily likeness (however appealing that became to some medieval artists) but the *gentleness* (and perhaps *innocency* cf. Mt 10.16) of the Spirit's descent. There is a contrast in Luke's writing between the Spirit's calm response to Jesus' prayer and the emphatic gale that engulfed the apostles on the day of Pentecost [Acts 2.1-4]. We are reminded that in Hebrew, whereas *ruach* is God's mighty wind, *nephesh* is his 'breath' – such as Jesus himself bestowed on his disciples gathered in Jerusalem on Easter evening:

> When he had said this, he breathed on them, and said to them, "Receive the Holy Spirit. [Jn 20.22]

The 'dovelike' movement of the Holy Spirit would thus seem to be the Father's way of confirming his Son's expression of humility. There is no reason to interpret the occasion, as some commentators have in time past, as God's *adoption* of Jesus as his Son (in theological language, 'an adoptionist christology', as contrasted with the Nicene Creed's presentation of Jesus as '*eternally* begotten' of the Father): rather, it endorsed the inner meaning of Jesus' Sonship, already known from his tenderest years, that he now fully appreciated after years of prayerful reflection upon the sacred scriptures.

Jesus' public ministry

Although Jesus' public ministry had been thus launched, a key issue inevitably arose concerning the overlapping role of John the Baptist: would the latter, for example, now retire gracefully from the scene altogether, assuming he did indeed recognise Jesus as 'the one who is mightier than I' [Mk 1.7]? It may be that Jesus was already aware of much displeasure directed against John by the public authorities, and had timed his visit accordingly – while popular acclaim was at its height, and before John's anticipated arrest.

Here it should not be forgotten that these were troubled times. In the 1st century there were a number of individuals who claimed a messianic role, or who might be seen in that light, most of whom (according to the Jewish writer Josephus, the chief source of historical information about this period of Judaean life) were seen as a threat by the ruling elite. Among them were opportunists such as Judas, son of Hezekiah (based at Sepphoris in Galilee), Simon (in Peraea) and a shepherd called Athrongaeus, 'whose hopes were based on his physical strength and contempt of death':

> He set a crown on his own head, but continued for a considerable time to raid the country with his brothers ... they were harassing all Judaea with their brigandage.

Sometimes these insurrections were responses to provocations by the Romans themselves; for example, the census 'when Quirinius was governor of Syria' [Lk 2.2] which was regarded as a direct challenge to God's own sovereignty; or the occasion when Pilate 'secretly and under cover conveyed to Jerusalem the [graven] images of Caesar' which certainly defiled the sanctity of the holy city. Claimants to the throne were not necessarily setting themselves up as 'Messiahs', but the general instability so engendered no doubt contributed to heightened messianic expectations.

Josephus mentions other figures who may have been perceived by some as messianic because of the prophetic mantle that they wore. These are found in his later work *Antiquities of the Jews*. There was, for example, Theudas [cf. Acts 5.36], who in the end was executed. He writes too of John the Baptist:

> Herod, who feared lest the great influence John had over the people might put it into his power and inclination to raise a rebellion (for they seemed ready to do anything he should advise), thought it best, by putting him to death, to prevent any mischief he might cause.

John's recorded location in the Jordan valley, not far from Qumran, makes it likely that he had some awareness of Essene teachings, which in several scrolls refer to a messianic being. However, a debate continues as to this Messiah's envisaged role, about which there is no apparent consistency: is he projected as a war leader, a prophet, a teacher of God's law, a ruler of the new Israel, a priest – or as God's agent would he be *sui generis*? John does not seem to identify any particular charism in his 'mightier' successor other than a baptism of Spirit and of 'fire'. Whether his preaching actually stirred up hopes of popular insurrection seems unlikely, but it was not long after his encounter with Jesus that he was arrested and imprisoned [Mk 1.14 cf. Matt 4.12; Lk 3.20], and like Theudas also put to death. The pretext for his execution was his apparent criticism of Herod's marriage to Herodias [Mk 6.17ff; Mt 14.3; Lk 3.19-20 – who adds '*and for all the evil things that Herod had done*']. Such outspoken comments would doubtless have been regarded as seditious and threatening; but, in fact, Mark seems to have been misled by popular rumour about Herod's family affairs (which were otherwise than he portrays), and he may have misrepresented the circumstances of John's arrest. Josephus's assessment that it was a political attempt to suppress an obviously popular movement seems more likely.

After Jesus' baptism 'the Spirit immediately drove him out into the wilderness' [Mk 1.12]. This provided time for further close communion with his Father and for reflection on the challenges lying ahead. The 'forty' days mentioned is not necessarily an exact count. In the Old Testament 'forty' is symbolic for a time of 'testing', as in the days and nights of rainfall that brought about the great flood [Gen 7.4], the years spent by the Israelite 'refugees' wandering in the Sinai peninsula, or the period of Elijah's retreat on Mount Horeb [1 Kgs 19]. Such examples remind us that the 'wilderness' could also be a place of refuge, and Jesus may have waited there until 'after John was arrested' [Mk 1.14 cf. Mt 4.12] in order to keep his own coming ministry quite separate from John's in the public mind.

On the other hand, Mark may have omitted a good deal of detail, for in the Fourth Gospel there are several early verses in which Jesus has already recruited his own disciples and begun baptising *before* John was put in prison [Jn 3.22-23; 4.1]: such details may have been included because of questions the evangelist was trying to answer about the origins of specifically *Christian* baptism? But John the Baptist's continuing activity [cf. Acts 19.1-4] leaves one wondering whether he had ceased to be quite so supportive of Jesus – and whether it indicated growing doubts about 'he who comes after me'? There is at least a useful clue here that Jesus may have moved up to Galilee from Judaea because he was not yet ready to face the inevitable onslaught from the strict Pharisaic party, who were now aware that he was 'making and baptising more disciples than John'. He had much work (of preaching and healing) to accomplish first. He also appreciated that it was religious opponents, rather than political figures, who would pose the greatest threat [cf. Jn 7.1, 30ff; 8.59; 10.31]; so, despite the seat of Herod's tetrarchy being at Tiberias, he clearly felt safer in the north.

Discrepancies between the Gospels leave us far from clear what Jesus' movements were after his baptism, and for how long his ministry actually lasted. But then none of the evangelists were intent upon writing his biography with chronological exactitude; rather, their task was to select and present coherently the mainly oral tradition that came to them. So Mark offers us a 'pilgrimage' that begins with Jesus in his native territory of Galilee, and ends with the events in Jerusalem that culminated in his death and resurrection; whereas John's schema depicts him going more than once to Jerusalem for a festival (which had after all been his long-standing custom), and then back to Galilee (and sometimes Samaria) again. The impression we therefore gain from Mark is of a shorter ministry, perhaps little more than a year, contrasted with about three years in John's reckoning – a more plausible figure.

Yet, although John, who writes later, has recourse to stories and sayings not found in the Synoptic Gospels which may be historically well-founded, it should not be assumed that John is invariably the most factually 'reliable' Gospel. What he records often carries symbolic themes that help to link the narrative together or to remind us of important ideas drawn from the Jewish tradition. For example, the 'days' referred to in his opening chapters seem to follow the pattern of revelation described in Exodus 19:

> And the Lord said to Moses, 'Lo, I am coming to you in a thick cloud, that the people may hear when I speak with you, and may also believe you for ever.' Then Moses told the words of the people to the Lord. And the Lord said to Moses, 'Go to the people and consecrate them today and tomorrow, and let them wash their garments, and be ready by the third day; for on the third day the Lord will come down upon Mount Sinai in the sight of all the people.'

Much can be drawn out of this – including its subsequent fulfilment on the 'third day' known as Easter – but we note here just the conclusion of the story of the wedding at Cana, which also happened on the third day:

> This, the first of his signs, Jesus did at Cana in Galilee, and manifested his glory; and his disciples believed in him.

A quick glance at any map of the Holy Land must surely dispel any idea that John's 'days' of chapters 2 and 3 are to be taken literally. Galilee is at the very least *several* days' walk from John the Baptist's location by the Jordan, reminding us that gospel itineraries are usually there to serve literary and theological purposes before anything else.

Indeed, despite their differences, what the four evangelists share in common is far more important. The Gospels were written as *testimony* to Jesus, and to his centrality in the life of Christian believers. The necessary selectivity of appropriate material and the purpose behind it are made most explicit in John's gospel:

> Now Jesus did many other signs in the presence of the disciples, which are not written in this book; but these are written that you may believe that Jesus is the Christ, the Son of God, and that believing you may have life in his name. [Jn 20.30-31]

Similar aims and methods are implicit in the other Gospels, which all begin in some way by introducing the reader to *who* Jesus was, and end with testimony to his *continuing life* [Lk 24.51] or *presence* [Mt 28.20]. The picture is somewhat clouded in Mark's case, since the ending of his Gospel is uncertain. It is arguable that Mark's intent was actually to point ahead to a more glorious meeting with the risen Lord who always 'goes before you'.

> Go, tell his disciples and Peter that he is going before you to Galilee; there you will see him, as he told you. [Mk 16.7]

Manifesting his glory

The suggestion here is that Jesus' self-awareness began at an early age and that his understanding of the divine mission yet to be accomplished deepened through years of prayer and scriptural reflection. It is surely no accident that, in Luke's Gospel, Jesus begins his ministry by preaching about the fulfilment of a text in Isaiah. Among all the Hebrew scrolls, this seems to have held the key to how he interpreted his coming role. It has sometimes been called the 'fifth Gospel' because, as Jerome once expressed it, the life of the Messiah is recounted in such a way as to make one think the prophet 'is telling the story of what has already happened rather than what is still to come'. The book of Isaiah is actually quoted in the New Testament more than any other book of the Hebrew scriptures apart from the Psalms: the fundamental reason for this is surely that this was the book that gave most guidance to Jesus during his so-called 'hidden years'.

It will be helpful to offer a brief survey of Isaiah's message. Although we now recognise historical development within the book as a whole, there are important common themes throughout, focusing on concepts such as God's holiness, and his desire for righteousness and faith, for peace and justice. Ritual purity and cultic practices are not enough in themselves, and indeed are condemned if they take the place of social justice [1.11-17; 58] or humility [66.1-4]. The Temple plays only a minor role in the vision of a new Jerusalem; in those passages where it is mentioned, the emphasis is on opening its doors to foreigners [56.3-8] and to the nations of the world [2.2-4; 66.18-21].

Visions of a new age often highlight an individual champion of justice and righteousness. This includes the passage quoted by Jesus in his 'manifesto' at Nazareth:

> The Spirit of the Lord is upon me, because he has anointed me to preach good news to the poor. He has sent me to proclaim release to the captives and recovering of sight to the blind, to set at liberty those who are oppressed, to proclaim the acceptable year of the Lord. [Lk 4.18-19 cf. Isa 61.1-4]

This prophetic model seems to underlie two other texts, in which he is described as 'the servant of the Lord' [49.1-6; 50.4-9], though in each case the reference may include Israel as an entity. But above all there is the celebrated 'suffering servant' passage, which seems to speak of an individual who heals and redeems by vicarious suffering [52.13-53.12]. It expresses confidence in the power of God to heal wounds and to forgive sins. The servant himself is not identified in Isaiah's text, which draws on traditional Jewish ideas such as the scapegoat ritual [53.4, 6, 12] and hints at the figure of Moses, who offered to die for his people [Exod. 32.32]. A reminder of God's past graciousness is found in the occasional use of wilderness motifs [e.g. 43.19-21; 48.21; 55.12-13].

The idea of 'service' is certainly suggested in Jesus' use of the term 'Son of man'. This phrase occurs repeatedly throughout the book of Ezekiel, where the prophet is addressed in this way; but it does occur once in Isaiah as well (although in parallel with the word 'man'):

> Thus says the Lord: 'Keep justice, and do righteousness, for soon my salvation will come, and my deliverance be revealed. Blessed is the man who does this, and the son of man who holds it fast.' [Isa 56.1-2]

Here the stress shifts from the phrase itself to the hastening of God's salvation by the implementation of his will. As that overworked modern cliché suggests, 'walking the talk' is an essential element in God's mission.

So it was that Jesus saw how his Sonship of the Father could fittingly be expressed, not just in the unpretentious phrase 'Son of man', but in a ministry of 'Isaianic' self-offering. The radiance of his divine glory was only to be found in the self-authenticating testimony of his love and compassion for others. St Paul explained this to the Philippians in words that may have been in use already as an early Christian hymn:

> [Christ Jesus], though he was in the form of God, did not count equality with God a thing to be grasped, but emptied himself, taking the form of a servant, being born in the likeness of men. And being found in human form he humbled himself and became obedient unto death, even death on a cross. [Phil 2.6-8]

It is also Paul, in letters that of course pre-date the Gospels, who offers an alternative term in place of Jesus' expression 'Son of man'. Adam, he writes to the Romans, was 'a type of the one who was to come' [Rom 5.14]: hence Jesus may be described as 'the new Adam'. Elsewhere, addressing the Church in Corinth, Paul uses the phrase 'the last Adam':

> For as in Adam all die, so also in Christ shall all be made alive … Thus it is written, 'The first man Adam became a living being'; the last Adam became a life-giving spirit. [1 Cor 15. 22, 45]

It is Christ as the new or last Adam who enables Christians themselves to attain 'to mature manhood, to the measure of the stature of the fulness of Christ' [Eph 4.13].

In subsequent writings of the early Fathers, it was above all Irenaeus who elaborated such teaching, particularly in his well-known line that Christ 'became what we are, that he might bring us to be even what he is himself'. More specifically, once again in his *Against Heresies*, Irenaeus sets out the basis of what later became known as 'recapitulation' theology:

> Therefore does the Lord profess himself to be the Son of man, comprising in himself that original man out of whom the woman was fashioned, in order that, as our species went down to death through a vanquished man, so we may ascend to life again through a victorious one.

In perhaps simpler terms, one might explain Christ as the true exemplar of how God intended us to live as human beings, created in his own image and likeness [Gen 1.26], which means in effect as 'the Man for others'. This is not a reduction to some form of humanism (a merely 'social' gospel), so long as we recall Irenaeus' important qualification:

> The glory of God is man fully alive, and the life of man is the vision of God.

Here we must return to the person of Jesus, whose life was given in compassionate service to bring hope and healing to others. Is it indeed possible to glimpse in his life a manifestation of divine glory? This was St John's claim, expressed in the prologue of his Gospel:

> And the Word became flesh and dwelt among us, full of grace and truth; we have beheld his glory, glory as of the only Son from the Father. [Jn 1.14]

Yet no manner of drawing comparisons, and no form of reasoning, can bring us to the core of Christian faith in Jesus as *Lord*. When Simon Peter professed him as 'the Christ, the Son of the living God', Jesus observed:

> Flesh and blood has not revealed this to you, but my Father who is in heaven. [Mt 16.17]

Of course, specific teachings of Jesus (which resonated with an aura of 'authority'), his miracles and acts of kindness, his personal disposition, the apparent resonances of his life with scriptural prophecies, his readiness to die for others and to forgive those who ill-treated him, and then his amazing resurrection, all contributed to people's perception of him. But even their combined weight could not 'prove' or infallibly reveal the secret of who he truly was. This is illustrated by the fact that at one point 'many of his disciples drew back and no longer went about with him' [Jn 6.66] and that at the last he was betrayed by Judas Iscariot. More striking though is the story of the future apostle Paul, who began as a fanatical and determined opponent of the new Christian movement – and no doubt knew much of Jesus' own record – yet who turned dramatically to faith on the Damascus road. It was not religious logic that prompted this, but a personal revelation.

The presentation of Jesus in the Temple
Russian icon 15th century

Jesus aged 12 disputing with the scribes
Book of Hours 15th century

The baptism of Jesus by John
William Blake 1803

The temptations of Jesus
Mosaic in St Mark, Venice 12th century

2. His social legacy

Life in the Spirit

Those who 'beheld' the fullness of divine 'grace and truth' in Jesus revered his teachings, which were not just spoken but frequently exemplified in his manner of life and his dealings with those he encountered. Paul is one of our earliest witnesses to the Church's intention to remain loyal to 'the Lord'. In his first letter to the Corinthians he addresses some of the questions that concern them, about which they had written. The whole of chapter 7 is devoted to marriage issues, and Paul's response is to start by considering the Lord's own guidance, which in his case Paul must have learnt at secondhand from the oral traditions in circulation: 'I give charge – not I, but the Lord'; 'To the rest I say, not the Lord'; 'Concerning the unmarried, I have no command of the Lord, but I give my opinion as one who by the Lord's mercy is trustworthy'. At the end of this chapter he suggests that his personal advice is trustworthy, since 'I think that I have the Spirit of God'.

It is certainly life in the Spirit that Paul commends. There were then many Christians who, like himself, came from a Jewish background, which by the 1st century provided detailed rulings about many aspects of life. How far were these rulings still important? In his letter to the Romans Paul offers a broad discussion of their pros and cons, but his conclusion is that 'in Christ Jesus' there is now a 'law of the Spirit of life' [Rom 8.2]:

> Now we are discharged from the law, dead to that which held us captive, so that we serve not under the old written code but in the new life of the Spirit. [Rom 7.6]

This adheres closely to what Jesus himself had taught:

> At that time Jesus declared, 'I thank thee, Father, Lord of heaven and earth, that thou hast hidden these things from the wise and understanding and revealed them to babes; yea, Father, for such was thy gracious will. All things have been delivered to me by my Father ... Come to me, all who labour and are heavy laden, and I will give you rest. Take my yoke upon you, and learn from me; for I am gentle and lowly in heart, and you will find rest for your souls. For my yoke is easy, and my burden is light'. [Mt 11.25-30]

The implied contrast here is with those who, like the Pharisees, 'bind heavy burdens, hard to bear, and lay them on men's shoulders' [Mt 23.4]. Jesus emphasises that his way is truly the Father's intention, in a passage where (unusually for a Synoptic Gospel) he speaks of his intimate relationship with the Father. We are reminded of the 'farewell discourses' in the Fourth Gospel, where Jesus explains to those whose 'learning curve' is now sufficiently advanced:

> The words that I say to you I do not speak on my own authority; but the Father who dwells in me does his works. [Jn 14.10]

The 'burden' mentioned by Matthew is elaborated further in John's text: the disciples are 'to love one another', to follow Jesus' example of 'washing one another's feet', and to witness faithfully to him despite persecution. We should also note an important rider concerning Jesus' teaching:

> I have yet many things to say to you, but you cannot bear them now. When the Spirit of truth comes, he will guide you into all the truth; for he will not speak on his own authority, but whatever he hears he will speak, and he will declare to you the things that are to come. He will glorify me, for he will take what is mine and declare it to you. [Jn 16.12-15]

The 'many things' yet to be understood would no doubt include the wisdom of those (like St Paul) who claimed to have 'the mind of Christ', although it rests with the faithful to discern whether such teachings are distinct from 'the wisdom of this age' and focus truly on 'Jesus Christ and him crucified' [1 Cor 2.2]. Interpretation of Jesus' words, as of the values he practised, is an ongoing process, which had already begun when the Gospels were written down; these embody the fruits of Christian reflection during the earliest decades. Their focus is clearly on the crucial events of Holy Week, which occupy several chapters in each of the Gospel narratives. Similarly, we should note that when Paul's credentials as an authentic apostle came under attack, whereas his earlier appeal [Gal 1-2] was to the recognition accorded him by the Jerusalem leaders 'of repute', he subsequently referred only to 'the things that show my weakness' [2 Cor 11.30]. Not least were his physical sufferings, so that he claimed to carry even in his body 'the death of Jesus' in order for the life of Jesus to be visibly manifested [2 Cor 4.10–11]. Indeed, his final plea to those who might still dispute his teaching was similar: 'Henceforth let no man trouble me; *for I bear on my body the marks of Jesus*' [Gal 6.17]. It was of course such marks still carried in Jesus' hands and side that enabled 'doubting Thomas' to recognise his risen Lord [Jn 20.27–28]. These marks of voluntary suffering were understood as summarising Jesus' core values.

The Church continues – as Jesus promised – to be led by the Holy Spirit 'into all the truth' [Jn 16.13]. The danger is that guidance relevant for one particular set of circumstances may be too rigidly retained even when the context has changed significantly. This is where Jesus' flexibility needs to be brought to mind. His concern was to bring liberty to the oppressed and to reach out to those who were marginalised, even if in so doing he appeared to transgress Jewish codes of behaviour. He was accused of being 'a glutton and a drunkard, a friend of tax collectors and sinners', which elicited the challenging comment, 'Yet wisdom is justified by her deeds' [Mt 11.19]. And in response to the accusation that his disciples had broken the Sabbath, he memorably replied:

> The Sabbath was made for man, not man for the Sabbath. [Mk 2.27]

Jesus was also aware that God's highest hopes and expectations are not necessarily fulfilled immediately. Human weaknesses and limitations may mean that we fail to realise God's real purposes; but we are not abandoned when we stumble. Several different examples from the Gospels spring to mind, as Jesus relates to people with varying degrees of 'acceptability':

- By the time Jesus sits down to eat the Last Supper with his disciples, it is already in Judas Iscariot's mind to betray him. Yet he is not expelled, but shares the meal with them all. Jesus even (in Matthew and Mark, but not in Luke or John) accepts his false kiss in the garden afterwards.
- Jesus requests a drink of water from the woman of Samaria, who has had five husbands already and is now living with another man altogether. He tells her that, if she had asked him, 'he would have given you living water' [Jn 4.10].
- Peter, who had earlier denied knowing Jesus, nevertheless professes love (*agape*) for him when they meet later by the Sea of Tiberias. He repeats this claim, and is 'grieved' to be asked again. Jesus accepts his

final response as perhaps more honest: Peter now restates his love as *philia* – affection, less demanding than the commitment implied in *agape*. Yet in the end he too would came 'to glorify God' by the manner of his death [Jn 21.19].

- Jesus urges caution in 'gathering up the weeds' prematurely [Mt 13.24-30]. The danger is that 'the wheat' may be uprooted at the same time – at an early stage it may be hard to distinguish between the two.

An enigmatic future

We need to recall that the inherited oral traditions used by the different evangelists were not all the same. The importance attached to particular issues may have varied in different places, which may therefore be reflected in the details or phraseology of particular *pericopes* or sayings. Material found in one Gospel may be wholly omitted in another, or found in a remarkably variant form. The influence of Old Testament passages may differ from one Gospel to another; and each evangelist no doubt had in mind a particular 'audience' for whom he was writing.

We have noted Jesus' frequent use of the phrase 'Son of man' as his preferred way of speaking about himself. In most instances it is clearly not a messianic title, but this seems to change in later chapters of the Synoptic Gospels where the end times are discussed and the *parousia* is prophesied:

> Then will appear the sign of the Son of man in heaven, and then all the tribes of the earth will mourn, and they will see the Son of man coming on the clouds of heaven with power and great glory; and he will send out his angels with a loud trumpet call, and they will gather his elect from the four winds, from one end of heaven to another. [Mt 24.30-31]

The imagery seems to be taken directly from the book of Daniel:

> I saw in the night visions, and behold, with the clouds of heaven there came one like a son of man, and he came to the Ancient of Days and was presented before him. And to him was given dominion and glory and kingdom, that all peoples, nations, and languages should serve him; his dominion is an everlasting dominion, which shall not pass away, and his kingdom one that shall not be destroyed. [Dan 7.13-14]

Yet is all this consistent with the temptations that Jesus rejected earlier?

> The devil took him to the holy city, and set him on the pinnacle of the temple, and said to him, 'If you are the Son of God, throw yourself down; for it is written, He will give his angels charge of you.' ... Again, the devil took him to a very high mountain, and showed him all the kingdoms of the world and the glory of them ... [Mt 4.5-6, 8]

It is almost as if Jesus' time of humble service on earth as 'Son of man' was subsequently considered (in some, but not all, circles) to have been ineffective; and so a 'second coming' with *power* and *great glory*, together with a company of *angels* – adjuncts that were deemed inappropriate at his first coming – is still necessary for God's kingdom to be fully established.

Of course, we are in the realm of imagery here, reassuring us that God's final victory is not in doubt. The early Church certainly needed to be reassured that the sacrifices of the faithful would not be in vain; so could it be that, when the Hebrew scriptures were scrutinised for messages of hope, the occurrence of the phrase 'Son of man' in Daniel was understood as referring to Jesus, prophesying the climax both of his story and of the world's; then, instead of remaining a poetic description of the End, a more literal version became embedded in the tradition and eventually in the (Synoptic) Gospels? Christian teaching about the Lord's coming clearly arose at an early stage, since Paul instructs the Thessalonians in similar terms well before the Gospels were composed. It was, he says, '*by the word of the Lord* that we who are alive, who are left until the coming of the Lord, shall not precede those who have fallen asleep.' His account continues as vividly as the Synoptic writings:

> The Lord himself will descend from heaven with a cry of command, with the archangel's call, and with the sound of the trumpet of God. [1 Thess 4.16]

Yet virtually none of this language occurs in John's Gospel. So the question arises: apart from speaking to his disciples of troubled times ahead, and therefore of their need to stand firm and if necessary to take up their own crosses (a warning found variously in all the Gospels), did Jesus also predict a 'second coming' in such apocalyptic language? How much of the latter was *by the word of the Lord*, given that the Fourth

Gospel presents a rather different future? In his farewell discourses Jesus announces that he is 'going to the Father' [Jn 16.10, 28] and will be seen no more. 'The Counsellor' (the Holy Spirit) will then be present 'for ever' with his disciples and will bring all his teaching to their remembrance. He himself will 'prepare a place' for them, indicating that 'he will *come again* and will take you to myself, that where I am you may be also' [Jn 14.3].

The manner of his coming is left unspecified in this Fourth Gospel: will it be a corporate or a personal visitation? C.K. Barrett suggests the following in his *Commentary*:

> The primary reference ... is to the eschatological advent of Jesus, or at any rate to his coming to the individual disciple at his death ... The ensuing discourse ... shows clearly that John's thought of the advent is by no means exhausted in the older Synoptic notion of the *parousia*. The communion of Jesus with his disciples, their mutual indwelling, is not deferred till the last day, or even to the day of a disciple's death.

So it is that in this Gospel we find a strong emphasis upon *eternal* life:

> God so loved the world that he gave his only Son, that whoever believes in him should not perish but have eternal life. [Jn 3.16]

> Whoever lives and believes in me shall never die. [Jn 11.26]

It is worth noting too Jesus' exchange with the crowd before Jesus' final Passover in Jerusalem:

> '*Now* is the judgment of this world, *now* shall the ruler of this world be cast out; and I, when I am lifted up from the earth, will draw all men to myself.' He said this to show by what death he was to die. The crowd answered him, 'We have heard from the law that the Christ remains for ever. How can you say that the Son of man must be lifted up? Who is this Son of man?' [Jn 12.31-34]

For John, the supreme moment of judgment is his Cross, which is simultaneously the revelation of his glory. It is a baffling idea to those who have not fully absorbed Jesus' stress upon messianic service, and his understanding that as the incarnate Son of the Father he fulfils this role most perfectly in his self-offering as 'Son of man'.

If, however, we argue that within the New Testament a mature appreciation of Jesus' teaching about what the future holds is expressed better among later writings such as the Fourth Gospel, we should also be aware that a vast literature exists that argues otherwise. The nature of the *parousia* is, one may safely say, as much an unresolved issue for us as it was for the early Church and for every generation of Christians ever since. It has become even more perplexing with the relatively recent growth in scientific understanding of the universe, which sees the prospect of life on earth quite differently from how it was regarded two thousand years ago. However, the phrase found in the Apocalypse, 'a new heaven and a new earth' [Apoc 21.1 cf. 2 Pet 3.13; Isa 65.17; 66.22], surely points beyond biblical literalism to a deeper spiritual understanding of what God has in store for our world.

The suggestion that later strands of the New Testament may be more helpful than apparently earlier texts in coming to understand Jesus' teaching may sound surprising, given that historians tend to give weight to the more 'original'. In science, of course, the reverse is usually true – newer theories that leave fewer unexplained observations come to supplant less satisfactory hypotheses. But with religious writings, and especially with prophetic material, something similar often happens. Divine revelation is a form of communication, requiring therefore its expression in language that – as far as possible – conveys its real meaning. This can well emerge gradually, under the guidance of the Holy Spirit – thus, scriptures old and new are ever open to fresh insights.

The key can often be to avoid reading 'difficult' texts in isolation (*'meaning'*, we were taught at Oxford by G. B. Caird, *'equals text plus context')* – so here the 'Son of man' sayings have been read alongside each other. Their context can be widened further by recalling that Jesus' future coming is not confined to the Last Day. The Gospels testify that he will be present under the forms of bread and wine in the Eucharist ('where two or three are gathered in my name'), anticipating the heavenly banquet – and prompting Jesus' disciples to live the new heavenly life even now. For what they do in acts of compassionate love (which is the keynote of heavenly existence) 'to one of the least of these my brethren' [Mt 25.40], is done to the Lord himself.

Authentic Christian living

As the Church grew both geographically and numerically, a key challenge was not merely to preach its faith in words but to express it in its internal life and in its self-presentation to the world. This was the challenge that Jesus posed to his disciples after James and John had sought to extract a promise of their own exalted position, 'one at your right hand, and one at your left, in your glory' [Mk 10.37]. In his reply Jesus laid out a blueprint for the Church's future institutional orientation:

> You know that those who are supposed to rule over the Gentiles lord it over them, and their great men exercise authority over them. But it shall not be so among you; but whoever would be great among you must be your servant, and whoever would be first among you must be slave of all. For the Son of man also came not to be served but to serve, and to give his life as a ransom for many. [Mk 10.42–45]

The same *pericope* is found with variations in the other synoptic writers, and it is essentially the same teaching in John's account of the feet-washing enacted by Jesus at the Last Supper:

> I have given you an example, that you also should do as I have done to you. [Jn 13.15]

It is evident even from the pages of the New Testament that this ideal was not invariably achieved. Paul could be over-assertive at times, most regrettably when he suggested to the Galatians that the 'circumcisers' should mutilate themselves [Gal 5.12]; or again, an overbearing attitude towards 'weak women' is apparent in the Pastoral Letters [2 Tim 3.6–7].

Yet as Paul saw it, the gospel is not a new 'law' ordering human affairs in a radically different way, even if that is one of its consequences: it is life 'in Christ', hence his own practical advice, given with 'the mind of Christ' [1 Cor 2.16; cf. 7.25, 40], is summed up not in a moral code but as the 'imitation' of Christ:

> Be imitators of me, as I am of Christ. [1 Cor 11.1]

This is not only the challenge for each Christian disciple, but it is also the chief requirement of the Church's leaders – those elders and overseers mentioned in the New Testament, whose ministry after initial decades of development evolved into that of bishops, priests and deacons. Jesus' essential commission to them, as to the Twelve, is to imitate his example of 'service', which implies willingness if needed for self-sacrifice. Such is Peter's advice to his 'fellow elders':

> Tend the flock of Christ that is your charge, not by constraint but willingly, not for shameful gain but eagerly, not as domineering over those in your charge but being examples to the flock. [1 Pet 5.2–3]

It is this self-forgetful concern for others that reminds believers of their Lord, enabling unbelievers too to glimpse Christ himself as the central meaning of the Church's life and faith. It can be particularly effective in male clergy, when the all-too-common experience of male dominance and aggression is replaced by humility and self-denial. Indeed, when persecution took its toll of the Church around the middle of the 3rd century, undergoing severe punishment – or even death – on account of one's faith came to be regarded as equivalent to priestly ordination. The so-called Canons of Hippolytus accepted that for such a man 'his confession is his ordination' [*Canon 6.43*]. In later years, roughly from the 5th century onwards, the marks of Jesus came to be symbolised in the particular hairstyle expected of the (Roman) clergy: the male tonsure, which represented Christ's crown of thorns (a reminder too of the martyr's crown worn in earlier times). Historically a shaven head in Greco-Roman society was the mark of a slave; clergy had dressed much as anyone else, with relatively short hair evident in frescoes and mosaics. Where Jerome had counselled 'modesty' as characterizing a priest's outward appearance [*Comm in Ezech 44*], the tonsure now placed a stronger emphasis on the presentation of Christ in his sacrificial humility. It was therefore pointedly countercultural.

Although there were notable exceptions, it was generally true that the majority of Christians in the early centuries came from poorer backgrounds. Pagan writers noted this disparagingly, but for the Church itself there was no shame in it. A prominent mark of Jesus' own ministry had been his frequent crossing of boundaries to include the poor and outcast, the 'unclean' and sinners, the marginalised, drawing criticism from the religious authorities. In Luke's account it was precisely these poor, along with those who hungered or wept or were persecuted for their convictions, who were blessed [Lk 6.20–23]. In practice, there might be lapses when class distinctions were not put to one side –

perhaps an almost inevitable consequence of meeting in a private house where family and slaves usually functioned separately. So Paul rebukes those at Corinth who 'humiliate' others with far less:

> When you meet together it is not the Lord's supper that you eat. For in eating, each one goes ahead with his own meal, and one is hungry and another is drunk. [1 Cor 11.20–21]

Exactly what was happening is not clear: the more affluent may have been arriving earlier than the workers, or they may have been bringing in food items which they were unwilling to share. Likewise, James complains of those who 'dishonour' the poor by discriminatory acts [Jas 2.6]. More appropriate behaviour, as commended by Jesus for 'a marriage feast', is to 'sit in the lowest place' [Lk 14.10]. Equally Jesus' teaching about the guest list for 'a dinner or a banquet' is relevant both to private hosts and to the patrons of house churches (several of those named in the New Testament being women):

> When you give a feast, invite the poor, the maimed, the lame, the blind. [Lk 14.14]

Paul gives expression to the same ethos when he writes to the Romans:

> Do not be haughty, but associate with the lowly. [Rom 12.16]

Those who are in various ways better endowed are urged 'not to think of [themselves] more highly than [they] ought to think' [Rom 12.3]. In the parable of the rich man and Lazarus, again recorded by Luke, it is the poor man neglected by the wealthy man who is 'carried by the angels to Abraham's bosom' when he dies [Lk 16.22]. Despite such possibly quite common failings of charity, the ideal of mutuality continued to be upheld: towards the end of the 2nd century, the apologist Athenagoras of Athens proudly reported the attendance of the uneducated, along with manual workers and old women, at Christian gatherings [*Legatio pro Christianis 11*].

When Paul returns the runaway slave Onesimus to his master Philemon, it is his hope that Onesimus will also be received as a brother Christian within his house church. Yet some slave owners could be harsh, perhaps of an unbelieving disposition [1 Pet 2.18]. Such texts therefore serve as reminders that while families and entire households may have become believers together, this was not invariably the case. The reiteration in the Synoptic Gospels of Jesus' warning to his followers about possible disruption of their family life [Mt 10.21,34–35,37; Mk 13.12; Lk 12.52–53; 14.26; 18.29; 21.16] is surely significant. The evangelists suggest that Christ knew something of this in his personal experience [Mt 12.46–50; Mk 3.21, 31–35; Lk 8.19–21; Jn 7.5]. Serious domestic difficulties may have arisen for believers who belonged to a household where the traditional family cult continued.

However, Mary herself is shown standing faithfully by Jesus' cross, where she is commended to the Beloved Disciple as his own mother too. Jesus' brothers likewise came to prominence in the Jerusalem church. So, while discipleship takes precedence over family ties [Mt 8.22; Lk 9.60] – in Luke's account even over commitments to one's 'wife' [Lk 14.26; 18.29] – they are by no means mutually exclusive. While Paul's comments about his own 'right' to be accompanied on his journeys by a wife (or literally 'a sister as wife') are not entirely clear, he seems to imply that all or most of the other apostles, along with the Lord's brothers, indisputably exercised such a right. He also gives encouragement to husbands and wives in 'mixed' marriages: a believer married to an unbeliever should allow that in time he or she may be the means of their spouse's salvation [1 Cor 7.16] – it seems to have been more common for Christian wives to have unbelieving husbands, rather than the reverse [1 Pet 3.1]. The children of any believer, according to Paul, are 'holy', even if their other parent does not share the faith [1 Cor 7.14].

Paul aside, it came to be expected of Christians in the early church that they should embrace the norm of marriage. Thus, 'the woman will be saved through bearing children' [1 Tim 2.15], with the same letter describing those who forbid marriage as 'liars whose consciences are seared' [1 Tim 4.2]. Paul reluctantly allows that those who have been widowed may marry again, but only a fellow Christian [1 Cor 7.39]. Yet the fact that the Pastoral Letters insist that *a church leader* must be 'above reproach, the husband of one wife' [1 Tim 3.2,12] rather suggests a lenience towards those in the flock who fell short of this ideal. To eschew marriage altogether was more widely encouraged only later, perhaps influenced by the knowledge of Jesus' own unmarried state – as Ignatius of Antioch suggests in his letter to Polycarp:

> Charge my brothers in the name of Jesus Christ to love their wives as Christ loves the Church. If somebody is capable of passing all his days in chastity, in honour of the Lord's body, let him do so. [*Ep Poly 5.2*]

In time, therefore, households (and house churches) eventually became of a more varied nature, possibly including consecrated virgins or other ascetics. The prime importance of asceticism was as a witness to heavenly realities, concerning which Jesus observed that 'they neither marry nor are given in marriage' [Mk 12.25]. Renunciation (not of course confined just to marriage!) served the positive purpose of pointing to the eventual transformation of all human life. Yet church tradition continued to respect marriage, an 'incarnational' engagement with the world of God's creating, alongside celibacy. Clement of Rome cautioned that, since 'to God we owe everything', there was no room for pride in one's particular calling, a warning re-iterated by Ignatius – '*anyone who boasts of his chastity is lost*'.

Extreme views were mainly the preserve of sects; yet by the 4th century it was not uncommon among the orthodox for renunciation to be preferred as 'the way of perfection'. This was advocated in the various Apocryphal Acts, which appealed particularly to devout upper-class ladies. Hence – aside from the burgeoning monastic movement – numerous lay ascetics might then be found in wealthy households. Since by this time martyrdom seldom occurred, role models of inspirational faith were sought elsewhere, and pressure for a celibate clergy continued to grow. However, the synod held in 340 at Gangra (Armenia) offered a rebuke:

> If any one shall maintain, concerning a married presbyter, that is not lawful to partake of the oblation when he offers it, let him be anathema. [*Synod of Gangra, Canon 4*]

The Church in these early centuries, we may conclude, upheld a 'mixed economy' – rich and poor, married and celibate, the strong and the weak, a gospel for the many, not the few.

Jesus as the Good Shepherd
Fresco in the Catacomb of St Callixtus, Rome 3rd century

Jesus casts out a devil
Wall-painting in St Sophia, Trebizond c. 1260

Jesus with the Samaritan woman
Mosaic in St Apollinare Nuovo, Ravenna early 6th century

Jesus raises Lazarus from the dead
Rembrandt c. 1630

3. His mission team

The variety of gifts

If Christians were well-advised not to imitate the practices and preoccupations of a dying order, they also needed to discover what Christ's 'new creation' meant both when they assembled together and in the direction of their personal lives. Certainly, love and mutual forbearance claim prominence within the body of Christ, as Paul recommended so fulsomely [1 Cor 12.31ff]. Luke's ideal, probably seldom attained, is that all who believe should have 'all things in common' [Acts 2.44; 4.32], with the concept of personal possessions now being abandoned. There is an exhortation by Jesus in the gospels to 'sell what you possess and give to the poor' [Mt 19.21; Mk 10.21; Lk 18.22], yet if some wealth and patronage had not been retained in apostolic times the Church's mission could not have developed as it did. Thus, distinctive roles remain, with Paul insisting that the variety of gifts can richly enhance the common good of each church. The apparently 'inferior' members have the greater honour, as James would readily agree – although his concern is restricted to disparities of wealth [Jas 2.1–7]. In the more affluent circumstances of Matthew's community, although the immediate application of Jesus' parable of the labourers may well have been to the respective contributions of Jew and Gentile, it is open to the further interpretation of valuing each person's contribution 'equally' [Mt 20.12] – and even of challenging householders to consider the implications for the management of their own affairs, to do 'whatever is right' [Mt 20.4].

The over-arching theme is that of 'mutual dependence', which applies also to the roles of men and women, and is poles apart from our contemporary insistence upon 'individualism' – each person claiming the right to do his or her 'own thing'. Thus, in Paul's words,

> In the Lord, woman is not independent of man nor man of woman;
> for as woman was made from man, so man is now born of woman.
> And all things are from God. [1 Cor 11.12–13]

Such a Christian partnership is well exemplified by Aquila and Prisca – who are also mentioned in reverse order: both Paul [Rom 16.3; 1 Cor 16.19] and Luke [Acts 18.18 cf. 18.2] refer to them.

Existing social conventions

Unfortunately, Paul's theological analysis gets entangled in practice with certain conventional social views. The traditions of the Church which he commends to the Corinthians include the fundamentals of Eucharistic worship, but also minutiae such as the hair coverings considered appropriate to the occasion. In arguing that women should cover their hair, his appeal is apparently first to the scriptural account of the sons of God gazing upon the daughters of men [Gen 6.2], then, even more weakly, to a lesson from 'nature itself', but in the end to the common practice of 'the churches of God' [1 Cor 11.16]. His ruling is therefore consistent with the advice he has just offered over the eating of food from the meat market: 'Let no one seek his own good, but the good of his neighbour'. A better rationale might therefore have been a more forthright observation such as, 'Nature teaches us – that men are easily distracted!' Nevertheless, there are doubts as to whether the life of the Spirit has not here been conformed to conservative propriety; in his letter to the Romans Paul presents a more radical challenge: to transform prevailing mental attitudes [Rom 12.2]. It is, however, claimed that by insisting on men praying bareheaded Paul was partially overturning customary expectations, given that *male* head covering was sometimes associated with a sense of social superiority.

Yet even if women's 'hair covering' is seen as an expression of the 'modest and sensible' attire required in the later Pauline tradition [1 Tim 2.9], we must still ask whether some inherited cultural attitudes have been perpetuated without justification. The most questionable assertion is that whereas man is 'the image and glory of God', woman is simply 'the glory of man'. The word 'image' is a reference to the book of Genesis, in which Paul relies upon the narrative of its second chapter to interpret the key text in chapter 1:

> God created man in his own image, in the image of God he created him; male and female he created them.

It was not until Augustine that a serious attempt was made [*De Gen ad Lit 3.22 cf. De Trin 12*] to reckon with the insistence here that woman too is in God's image:

Some people have suggested that it was now [Gen 1.27] that the human mind was made, while the human body came later, when scripture says, 'And God fashioned man from the dust of the earth' [Gen 2.7]; so that where it says 'he made' [1.26], it refers to the spirit, while 'he fashioned' [2.7] refers to the body. But they fail to take into account that male and female could only be made with respect to the body. While indeed it may be acutely argued that the human mind, in which the human being is made to God's image and which is a kind of rational life, has two functions: the contemplation of eternal truth and the management of temporal affairs; and that thus you get a kind of male and female, the one part directing, the other complying; it is still the case that the mind is only rightly called the image of God in that function by which it adheres in contemplation to the unchangeable truth. It is to symbolize or represent this point that the apostle Paul says that it is only the man who is the image and glory of God; 'but the woman', he says, 'is the glory of the man'. [1 Cor 11.7]

Thus, Augustine begins to undermine Paul's expression of male supremacy; what he offers is an allegorization in which male and female are, at least in this passage, features of human rationality – which belongs to men and women alike. Even so, he considers it fitting that the directing element is 'a kind of male', and the complying element correspondingly female; the terminology here relies more upon customary usage rather than upon theological chauvinism.

In his first letter to the Corinthians (which may in its present form be composite), Paul has further, somewhat inconsistent, words about the possible contribution of women in Christian worship. His discussion of headgear occurs within the context of how men and women should prophesy or pray in the gathered assembly; but subsequently there is a blanket prohibition of women even speaking at all:

> As in all the churches of the saints, the women should keep silence in the churches. For they are not permitted to speak, but should be subordinate, as even the law says. [1 Cor 14.34]

Some have taken the phrase 'to speak' as meaning either 'to argue' or 'to chatter', but the more plausible reading is to see this as a subsequent interpolation (variously placed in early manuscripts), arising from what struck some at least as unseemly behaviour. While it is uncharacteristic of Paul to appeal to 'the law' for resolution of an issue, if there were Jewish Christians in Corinth who considered that the active participation of women in worship was contrary to the passive role expected of them in the synagogue, he might have felt it expedient to prevent a split developing. We note that when writing to the Romans he tactfully expressed a more appreciative view of the law than in his much earlier correspondence with the Galatians – although even there, while arguing against the imposition of circumcision upon the Gentiles, he did not press home the logic that Jewish Christians should abandon it too. At the very least it appears that Paul's ruling was designed to keep the peace, and to avoid a contentious split within the Church, 'For God is not a God of confusion but of peace [1 Cor 14.33]'.

A related issue appears in the reference to the impact on 'outsiders or unbelievers' [1 Cor 14.23] of what happens in the Church's worship. This seems to have been a time when house churches were ceasing to be domestic gatherings, and becoming more open to visitors or God-seekers. Paul insists that all things should be done for 'edification' [1 Cor 14.27], and some outsiders might well have found a more active participation of women both an unfamiliar and also a somewhat 'shameful' spectacle. This is a perennial issue for the Christian Church: a 'word' proclaimed – whether through a celebration of worship, a teaching of faith, an act of witness – needs to be a 'word' that is in some measure received, or else communication has failed. In transforming human life, God's coming kingdom is not so radical that present hopes and values are wholly overturned, but neither are they left intact. There has to be change, but as John Henry Newman once so aptly expressed it:

> What the genius of the Church cannot bear is, changes in thought being hurried, abrupt, violent – out of tenderness to souls, for unlearned and narrow-minded men get unsettled and miserable. The great thing is to move all together and then the change, as geological changes, must be very slow.

Newman observed that the outcome of such charitable concern was often the counter-accusation of 'duplicity'. Yet Paul's apparent inconsistencies may be understood as deriving, not from any such double-mindedness, but from the hierarchy of values which are expressed more than once in this same letter. Without love, he writes, 'I am a noisy gong or a clanging cymbal ... I am nothing ... I gain nothing' [1 Cor 13.1–3]. Or again, he warns:

> Take care lest this liberty of yours somehow becomes a stumbling block to the weak ... wounding their conscience when it is weak, you sin against Christ. [1 Cor 8.9, 12]

Complementary roles

There are nevertheless various passages in the Gospels and in Acts which challenge Paul's ambiguous message about women. In the days preceding Pentecost, the embryo house church is gathered for prayer in the Upper Room in Jerusalem. Along with the eleven disciples Luke lists the presence of 'the women and Mary the mother of Jesus' and 'his brothers'. The decision is then taken to replace Judas Iscariot with a twelfth disciple, who must have been with the Lord from the time of his baptism to his ascension, as a fellow 'witness to his resurrection'. This is therefore no random assembly, but a gathering of *witnesses*, in which women play an essential complementary role to the men. Prior to the crucifixion most of the apostles had apparently gone into hiding, since the Gospels largely omit them from the scene; Luke refers in his account only to Jesus' 'acquaintances' being present alongside 'the women who had followed him from Galilee' [Luke 23.49], while John tells us only of the Beloved Disciple being at their side. Mary of Nazareth witnessed in addition his birth, his childhood, his upbringing and much more: Mary of Magdala was certainly a witness to his resurrection. We may conclude that, regardless of any church offices that emerged later, men and women were alike valued as *Christian witnesses.* As well as their vital personal knowledge of the Lord, the later sacrifices made by women were equally valuable testimony to Christian faith. Luke notes that when 'believers were added to the Lord' there were 'multitudes both of men and women' [Acts 5.14] – and that both alike suffered arrest and imprisonment [Acts 8.3; 9.2].

The complementarity of men and women within the Christian perspective is expressed in other ways as well. While Jesus was still in Mary's womb, it was Elizabeth who 'was filled with the Holy Spirit' and rejoiced in her visitation by 'the mother of my Lord' [Lk 2.41-45]. Shortly after Christ's birth he was presented in the Temple at Jerusalem, encountering both Simeon and his counterpart the 'prophetess Anna' [Lk 2.36]; they spoke in turn farsightedly about his future role. We read later too of the 'four unmarried daughters of Philip the evangelist who prophesied' at Caesarea [Acts 21.9]; thus, for Luke, the gift of *prophecy* is seen as equally available for men and women:

> In the last days it shall be, God declares, that I shall pour out my Spirit upon all flesh, and your sons and your daughters shall prophesy ... and on my menservants and my maidservants in those days I will pour out my Spirit; and they shall prophesy. [Acts 2.17–18 cf. Mt 10.41]

If Paul's concern for 'edification' has led him to restrict the role of women in church worship, it is not that he differs from Luke in appreciating their partnership with men in the wider mission of the Church; indeed, 'the body is one and has many members' [1 Cor 12.12]. From his own upbringing he would have appreciated that Jewish faith was centred not on the synagogue but on the home, where it was women who maintained the household. There is no suggestion, however, that their ministry is solely a domestic affair, vital though it had been in Jesus' life [Luke 8.1–3] and important as it remained [Tit 2.3–4]. Paul does not differ from Jesus in his readiness to see women as his fellow-workers for the gospel. In John's gospel both the woman at the well and Mary Magdalene in the garden (their male counterparts being, respectively, Nicodemus and Thomas) leave their encounter with Jesus to *evangelize* their acquaintances. So too Paul commends a number of his 'sisters' for their Christian work: Phoebe [Rom 16.1], Mary [Rom 16.6], Tryphaena and Tryphosa [Rom 16.12], Euodia and Syntyche [Phil 4.2] among them, with Thecla also prominent in subsequent non-canonical literature linked to the name of Paul. St Clement of Rome in his turn gives favourable mention to the courageous faith of 'the blessed Judith' and to Esther's 'humbleness of spirit'; they were to be reckoned among 'the females [who] have frequently been enabled by God's grace to achieve feats of heroism' [*1 Clem 55*].

Yet there is still a hint in the Fourth Gospel of a role for women that has never fully germinated. The role model of greatest significance for all Christians is that of Jesus himself, but in the Church's authorized ministry attention is more often drawn to the fact that the Twelve appointed by him as his apostles were men, and not women. The question arises: does this necessitate that those who succeed them in ministry must – like them – always be male? It is generally argued in the Catholic Church that there is no authority to do otherwise, but this seems to overlook:

- the fact that within a generation Paul enabled non-Jews (albeit not without considerable opposition at first) to participate fully in the life of the Church (including its ministry), despite Jesus' initial restriction of his Twelve to those who were practising Jews;
- the promise of our Lord to continue guiding his Church through the power and wisdom of the Holy Spirit;
- the conferring of his authority to take decisions 'about anything they ask' [Mt 18.19], provided it is appropriately 'agreed' (thus, the incorporation of non-Jews was formally approved at the so-called Council of Jerusalem, as described by Luke);
- the sacramental developments of later centuries (affecting initiation, penance and marriage in particular), which indicate that the Church was prepared to use its devolved authority.

A weightier reason for restricting ordination to men surely lies in the fact that Jesus himself was male. What symbolic significance does this hold? When a priest stands at the altar, in some way he represents Christ to the congregation. Is it the maleness, or the humanity, of Jesus that counts? A theology that stresses incarnation will perhaps say that Christ's humanness is all-important; one that looks to the Cross will see there a work of redemption accomplished very much by a male who is passive and forgiving in the face of masculine aggression and violence. Here we may find guidance in the message spelt out by Jesus in his 'farewell discourse', on the occasion of the Last Supper. He was aware of those among his disciples like the sons of Zebedee who were ambitious for their own status within his coming kingdom, and in a dramatic counter-play he stooped down to wash all their feet [Jn 13.2-17]. He left no room for doubt in his subsequent comment:

> If I then, your Lord and Teacher, have washed your feet, you also ought to wash one another's feet.

Yet John has already shown us such an action earlier in his gospel, when Mary of Bethany 'took a pound of costly ointment of pure nard and anointed the feet of Jesus and wiped his feet with her hair; and the house was filled with the fragrance of the ointment' [Jn 12.3]. So, if ministry is, as Jesus suggests, not about power and authority but essentially a task of *service*, may we not see in the Bethany incident a potential for women to share in the role? Just as Jesus' various encounters with Gentiles in his own earthly ministry paved the way for the fuller engagement of the apostolic Church in Paul's time, may we not see our Lord's acceptance of Mary's service as a sign that he would sanction the fuller incorporation of women into the Church's ministry as and when 'the time was ripe'?

We need of course to exercise considerable caution: there is in the Church's ministry a significantly different emphasis from that which often obtains in the secular world, where women have now been liberated in many ways (well beyond the landmark step of including them within the universal franchise). We are accustomed to female heads of state, female managing directors, female doctors and so on. We accept that women are just as capable as men at most jobs. But 'ministry' is not just a job or a series of jobs – as in preaching sermons, saying mass, visiting the sick, or running a parish. Nor is it simply about heading up and representing an institution. The pastor (meaning here 'an ordained person') is there to articulate the common calling of all God's people and to remind them of their vocation – a task fulfilled not merely by words and actions. At heart it is about focusing in one's self the truth revealed in Jesus Christ, for whom the Church exists. The key, Jesus expresses variously, is 'loving service' or 'dying to self' or 'taking up one's cross' but certainly not in 'self-assertion'. In fulfilling such a role, gender seems largely irrelevant: in Paul's words (whose implications he only partially followed through?),

> There is neither Jew nor Greek, there is neither slave nor free, there is *neither male nor female*; for you are all one in Christ Jesus. [Gal 3.28]

Yet there may be remaining doubts, not about the person of Christ as representing our common humanity (once again in Pauline language as 'the new Adam') rather than as simply the male gender; but as one who shares God's divine nature:

> No one knows the Father except the Son and any one to whom the Son chooses to reveal him. [Mt 11.27]

Indeed, Jesus teaches us to address God as "Our Father", although there are passages elsewhere in the Bible which introduce some feminine imagery. Thus, in Isaiah God is likened to a mother bearing or suckling or comforting her child. In the Psalms God is a midwife and is also compared to a mother bird – perhaps reminiscent of the language used to depict Moses' ark, where 'the cherubim spread out their wings above, overshadowing the mercy seat with their wings' [Exod 37.9]. But that is precisely the point: we are talking in metaphors and similes, in poetic imagery which evokes powerful religious ideas. Hence it trivializes the discussion to speak of God crudely as male or female. The terms used are not so much masculine and feminine as words which tell us the kind of *relationship* in which we stand to God. As persons, our two most fundamental human relationships are with our father and with our mother. They are different in kind, characterized, at least in the early stages, by closeness to our mother (who offers us warmth and security) and by distance from our father (who makes demands upon us and so awakens us to a rather wider world). We experience God in a similar twofold way, as immanent and close but also as transcendent, over against us, the moral God of monotheistic faiths. This latter feature is of course strongly portrayed in the Old Testament in the prophetic tradition. Yet it needs careful qualification. If God is only the Almighty, the King, the Judge, the Lord of hosts, perhaps he threatens to destroy us? Hosea wrestled with this question and sought to introduce a more tender note, but the dilemma is not resolved until we reach the New Testament. *In Jesus God is 'father and mother' at once.* As he reaches out in prayer to his Father in heaven, he points us to the source of our being; in his sacrificial love he reveals the compassion and the tenderness of God, those 'feminine' qualities. Jesus, the image of the unseen God, shows us the Almighty stooping low, the power and authority of God surrendering itself on the Cross. Here is the role model with which pastors of the Church are called to identify – irrespective of their gender. So, if Mary of Bethany stoops low to anoint the Lord's feet in humble service, it is because (according to Luke) she had first sat there 'and listened to his teaching' – just as Mary, mother of Jesus, had also 'kept all these things, *pondering them in her heart'*.

The evidence gleaned thus far from the days of the early Church is that women were then already appreciated as *witnesses* to the gospel (indeed, as active *evangelists*), as *prophets* and as exemplars of *service*, quite apart from their role in hosting house churches. There may even be a hint in Luke's gospel in the pairing of Jesus' parables of the Lost Sheep (recovered by a male shepherd) and the Lost Coin (for which a woman searched diligently) that men and women are equally fitted for *pastoral* roles. It should be recalled here that, when Paul (or perhaps one of his colleagues) wrote to the Ephesians, he described Christ's gifts to the Church as follows:

> Some should be apostles, some prophets, some evangelists, some pastors and teachers, to equip the saints for the work of ministry, for building up the body of Christ. [Eph 4.11-12]

It would seem indisputable that such gifts were not the sole preserve of men.

Later developments

However, in post-apostolic times the Church's ministry developed rather differently, with the 'threefold order' of bishops, presbyters and deacons assuming centre stage, perhaps through the influence of Jerusalem's own leadership structure in which 'elders' i.e. presbyters were initially more prominent: they are mentioned in many of the later New Testament writings as well as in Acts, and subsequently in *1 Clement* and the *Didache*. Thus, the Pauline 'charismatic' schema came to be supplanted: and, although women were still very much part of the Christian community, they took little part in these leadership roles. Notwithstanding his aforementioned appreciation of those who displayed outstanding zeal, Clement of Rome's usual expectation is that Christian women should be 'patterns of discretion in every way', which included 'the self-restraint of their tongues by observing silence' in church [*1 Clem 1.3; 21.7*]; but – as with Paul – this appears to be conventional seemliness. It was also customary in Greco-Roman society for men and women to be segregated on public occasions, such as at banquets or at the circus, and it seems likely that both synagogues and church assemblies came to adopt this practice during the 1st century. The *Apostolic Tradition* records the custom that was then established:

> Women, whether believers or catechumens, shall stand for their prayers by themselves in a separate part of the church. [*Ap Trad 18*]

The 3rd century document *Didascalia Apostolorum* has more detail about what was then required in Syrian church gatherings for 'decent order' to be maintained:

> In the most easterly part of the house the presbyters sit with the bishops, next the lay men, and then the women; so that when you stand up to pray, the leaders may stand first, and after them the lay men, and then the women too. [*Did Apost 2.57*]

This account leaves it uncertain as to whether or not women contributed vocally in the prayers.

While there is a hint of women deacons in the Pastoral Letters [1 Tim 3.11], any ministry they exercised would have been limited to the needs of their own sex [1 Tim 2.12]. It is now generally agreed that, in the early centuries, they assisted at baptisms and at the anointing of women who were sick – and if complaints were made to the bishop from women who were brutally treated by their husbands it would have been women deacons who inspected the resultant bruises and scars. There is thus a firm precedent for ordaining women to the diaconate.

There were sometimes problems, of course, with women exercising public roles. Thus, 'Jezebel' was a self-styled prophetess at Thyatira whom John criticizes for leading people astray [Apoc 2.20]. Yet such complaints were directed no less to men as well, and there are warnings in the New Testament about those who would cause damage through their ministrations. In Paul's words

> I know that after my departure fierce wolves will come in among you, not sparing the flock; and from among your own selves will arise men speaking perverse things, to draw away the disciples after them. [Acts 20.29-30]

And although Jesus himself found it necessary to issue rebukes, which are found throughout the gospels; these also apply more often to men than to women.

A reasonable conclusion is that, as women came to assume different roles from men within the Church, it was not principally because they lacked the required gifts but because their prominence was socially problematic. That is arguably no longer true in many of today's cultures, and therefore opens the door to further 'inculturation' which has been a guiding principle of the Church's mission down the ages (here may be recalled Paul's confession that he became 'all things to all men, that I might by all means save some'). Change – allowing a more inclusive ministry – may be thought desirable within the Catholic Church, but it would certainly be controversial and would (as Newman warned) take considerable time and patience.

In the early 1990s the Church of England made the decision to proceed with women's ordination, but the crucial vote was only narrowly won and the debates that preceded it paid scant regard to significant Christian opinion elsewhere – such as in the worldwide Anglican Communion, or in the Catholic and Orthodox Churches. This resulted, not only in further Anglican divisions, but in a major setback to wider unity talks which until then had made much progress over the previous two or three decades. It seemed as if our Lord's devout prayer 'that they may be one, even as we are one' [Jn 17.11] was being disregarded.

However, it is possible to regard the Anglican innovations as a 'pilot scheme', which might in time enable similar moves in the Catholic Church to proceed more circumspectly, aware of the risks entailed. There is, for example, a strong wave of secularization sweeping across the Western world, with far fewer younger people engaging with the churches or professing any kind of religious faith; yet among young men there are instances of those who turn to Islam as a way of asserting a more 'masculine' (or 'macho') identity, which might suggest caution in opening doors of ministry to women, given its possible misinterpretation as a 'feminizing' of Christianity. Given that many churches, in any case, already experience a preponderance of women, would this tendency simply be boosted further; indeed, might women's ordination result in a significant diminution of priestly vocations among men?

Nevertheless, the times are changing, and the call of mission is urgent. In Elizabethan England there was discussion in recusant Catholic circles as to how far radical measures might be needed in their *modus operandi*: there were those who considered that established patterns of ministry were inadequate in their current situation. It might be argued similarly today that the traditional institutional ministries need to be supplemented by the more varied charismatic roles known to St Paul, some of which were certainly fulfilled by women with the appropriate gifts. If the *ressourcement* sought in the 2nd Vatican Council of the 1960s is to serve the Church's *aggiornamento*, the Holy Spirit may be prompting us once again to appreciate the charisms that women can offer – whether within the historical threefold order or alongside it. In one of the Council's keynote documents *Lumen Gentium* (i.e. Christ as 'the light of the nations') we are reminded:

> The Church, which the Spirit guides in way of all truth and which he unified in communion and in works of ministry, he both equips and directs with hierarchical and charismatic gifts and adorns with his fruits. By the power of the Gospel he makes the Church keep the freshness of youth ... It is not only through the sacraments and the ministries of the Church that the Holy Spirit sanctifies and leads the people of God and enriches it with virtues, but, allotting his gifts to everyone according as He wills, He distributes special graces among the faithful of every rank. By these gifts He makes them fit and ready to undertake the various tasks and offices which contribute toward the renewal and building up of the Church, according to the words of the Apostle: "The manifestation of the Spirit is given to everyone for profit". These charisms, whether they be the more outstanding or the more simple and widely diffused, are to be received with thanksgiving and consolation for they are perfectly suited to and useful for the needs of the Church. [*LG* 1.4; 2.12]

An impressive example of an innovative ministry has recently developed in Zimbabwe, where a significant proportion of the population now suffer from stress, depression and mental illness, and find the 'friendship bench' an invaluable help: the *voluntary counsellors* are local African grandmothers. Another (global) initiative has been the calling of young people to serve in areas of unrest as *peace agents*, promoting not only reconciliation but inner spiritual peace.

Historic developments of Christian ministry do not necessarily bind today's Church to reproducing only the models that have served well in the past – and it is worth recalling, given the shortage of priests in some areas of the world, that there have been times when 'lay' celebration of the eucharist might have been feasible. John Moschos recorded in the late 6th century that at Choziba Monastery near Jerusalem a lay brother 'bringing the oblations recited the holy prayer of offering on the way' and 'an angel of the Lord' declared them thereby to have been 'consecrated and made perfect' – but Abba John (later a bishop) stepped in to rule against this happening again (nobody was to learn the prayer unless he had been ordained)!

It is important not to restrict discussion of vocation to currently familiar roles, but to be imaginative about the opportunities for Christian mission and service in the constantly developing circumstances of the present day. For his part, Pope Francis is presently assessing the possibility of reviving the ordination of women as deacons – a move taken recently by the Orthodox Patriarch of Alexandria. Yet, while issues of 'equality' and the recognition of women's undoubted gifts remain important both for Christians and for our contemporaries, other considerations matter too: the Lord prayed for unity (not bitter wrangling) among his followers, so as to enable them to reach beyond 'political correctness' and to implement his vision of divine healing for all the world's brokenness. The aim of true 'reformation' is to further the coming of God's kingdom, 'on earth as it is in heaven'.

In a more inclusive Church, gifts described by Paul as 'varieties of working' [1 Cor 12.4-12], should be widely encouraged. The furtherance of roles for women might help to promote his appreciation that Christ's body 'does not consist of one member but of many' [1 Cor 12.14] and thus also to enable better collaboration between clergy and laity – bearing in mind that both 'clericalism' and 'careerism' have damaged the Catholic Church very considerably in recent decades. Rather than emphasizing the customary structures of the Church, today's focus (in the Western world at least) should be upon Christ's *mission* regaining spiritual momentum. The word 'church', after all, can well be understood better as more of a verb than a noun – not just a movement but (to use Pope John Paul II's description) a mover and a shaker!

Jesus' entry into Jerusalem
Giotto in the Scrovegni Chapel, Padua c. 1304

Jesus at the Last Supper
Fragment of Coptic silk-embroidered linen 6th century

Jesus before Pilate
Tintoretto in Scuola Grande di San Rocco, Venice 1567

Jesus crucified
Via Crucis in St Louis Montfort, Balaka, Malawi 1994

4. His cultural embrace

Unity and diversity

A key moment in the life of the early Church has already been mentioned – the Council of Jerusalem, which released Gentile Christians from some of the requirements of the Jewish Law:

> It has seemed good to the Holy Spirit and to us to lay upon you no greater burden than these necessary things: that you abstain from what has been sacrificed to idols and from blood ('*and from what is strangled*' is added here in some manuscripts, although somewhat unnecessarily given that *blood* would have remained within the flesh of a strangled beast) and from unchastity. [Acts 15.28-29]

By this decree St Paul's mission to the predominantly pagan coastlands of the Mediterranean was enabled to continue without endangering the unity of the Church. Indeed, it was faithful to Christ's own practice of mixing with 'publicans and sinners', and generally reaching out beyond the bounds of conventional propriety. It is always God's love and his mercy that are fundamental, and when these are expressed within any code of Christian belief or practice it is vital that too narrow or too rigid an interpretation is avoided. Inevitably perhaps, there will always be those who claim that their preferred version of the gospel is the only one that is acceptable, or that their particular forms of worship must be observed universally, or that their ecclesiastical structures are uniquely sanctioned; but the truth embodied in St James' edict of 50 AD (or thereabouts) is that unity is far more essential to the Church than uniformity.

Paul encountered other divisive issues, apart from his clash with the 'circumcision party' at Antioch [Gal 2.11-12]. There were significant dissensions at Corinth:

> I appeal to you, brethren, by the name of our Lord Jesus Christ, that all of you agree and that there be no dissensions among you, but that you be united in the same mind and the same judgment. For it has been reported to me by Chloe's people that there is quarreling among you, my brethren. What I mean is that each one of you says,

> "I belong to Paul," or "I belong to Apollos," or "I belong to Cephas," or "I belong to Christ." [1 Cor 1.10-12]

Factions such as these became alas! all too common in the years (and the centuries) that followed. Sometimes there were teachings or practices that departed significantly from Christian norms and certainly needed to be challenged: those who propagated them are described in the pages of the New Testament as 'deceivers' [2 Jn 7]. At other times the issues may have been clouded by personal vanities that put self before Christ: Diotrephes, mentioned in the 3rd Letter of John, seems to have caused division by refusing to acknowledge any authority beyond himself. Such sad developments could only emphasize the unifying role of Peter (or his successor) as the Church's 'rock', and it may be that the problems caused by such as Diotrephes were in mind when chapter 21 was added as a later appendage to the Fourth Gospel. Here we read of seven disciples (symbolic of the whole body) fishing on the Sea of Tiberias (or Galilee) after Easter; their catch was hauled ashore to Jesus by Simon Peter himself.

> The net [was] full of large fish, a hundred and fifty-three of them; and although there were so many the net was not torn. [Jn 21.11]

The background context provides a possible interpretation of the opening number '153'. In line with the near-contemporary text, the *Letter of Barnabas*, where the number 318 of Abraham's followers is deciphered digit by digit (3 is taken as T, the sign of the Cross and 18 as IH, which begins Jesus' name in Greek), so here 1 may stand for 'unity' or again for 'Jesus', while 5 and 3 may indicate the different Jewish and Gentile ethical requirements (the five books of the Law, and the three requirements in the decree of Acts 15). The point, at any rate, is that the mixed catch of fish did not tear the net (the Church) apart.

In the following verses pastoral care of the Christian flock is entrusted to Peter; Jesus hints that his responsibilities will be challenging, but while he warns Peter about approaching ordeals, he leaves the Beloved Disciple's future uncharted – 'what is that to you?' he asks Peter. Peter has, of course, just been 'reinstated' – forgiven and reassured of the Lord's love after his triple denial in the High Priest's courtyard. Yet his tendency to waver at times has not disappeared altogether. We observe that after his principled clash with Paul at Antioch, he reverted to the same position himself, which Luke indicates [Acts 10] he had reached earlier through his vision at Joppa and its subsequent confirmation at Caesarea. He had then been called to defend his actions [Acts 11.1-18] and so – when the situation at Antioch was brought before the Council of Jerusalem – he was the obvious spokesman for the Gentiles' cause. To our surprise, it was then James, the Lord's brother [Acts 15.19 cf. Gal 1.19] who pronounced the final verdict; Paul refers to him as an 'apostle', but he was not even one of the original Twelve. So, despite Peter's primatial calling, authority in the early Church was exercised in a more collegial manner: Peter was prepared to listen to others, to seek their wisdom and guidance, and even to submit to their judgment. Perhaps he recognized that in discerning God's will, despite the guidance of the Holy Spirit through 'trances' and dreams, he himself might on occasion be influenced by other factors as well, and needed the support of the whole Church. As John expressed it in his 1st Letter:

> Beloved, do not believe every spirit, but test the spirits to see whether they are of God. [1 Jn 4.1]

In 'testing the spirits' as the Church's leaders did at Jerusalem, they were surely heeding Jesus' counsel that they should not 'lord it' over others [e.g. Mt 20.25] and were truly following his example of humility. In fact, although Simon Peter is designated 'the rock' and receives the keys of the kingdom of heaven [Mt 16.19], Jesus indicates that such authority is on occasion shared by others too [Mt 18.18].

An early example of 'collaborative' ministry occurs at the beginning of Acts, when a replacement is sought for Judas Iscariot among the Twelve. Peter spoke first, setting out the guidelines, but then invited nominations from the assembled company (numbering one hundred and twenty) and finally left the choice to God through the casting of lots. John Chrysostom, Patriarch of Constantinople, commented on the process in one of his homilies:

> He allowed the multitude to choose, and so secured honour for those who were elected, and avoided any ill-feeling that might have arisen against himself. For great matters like this often have evil effects. Did Peter then not have the right to choose? Certainly, he had the right,

but he refrained from exercising it in case he might seem to be guilty of favouritism ... He did not put forward (the names) himself, but all did so together. It was he who made the suggestion, pointing out that it was not his own, but came from an old prophecy. So he was interpreting, not giving orders.

There have been times, as we know from historical records, when the task of discernment within the Church has been exercised too hastily, without the necessary insight and patience that characterized Christ's own ministry. One of the parables recorded by Matthew warns against this (as noted previously):

> The kingdom of heaven may be compared to a man who sowed good seed in his field; but while men were sleeping, his enemy came and sowed weeds among the wheat, and went away. So when the plants came up and bore grain, then the weeds appeared also. And the servants of the householder came and said to him, 'Sir, did you not sow good seed in your field? How then has it weeds?' He said to them, 'An enemy has done this.' The servants said to him, 'Then do you want us to go and gather them?' But he said, 'No; lest in gathering the weeds you root up the wheat along with them. Let both grow together until the harvest; and at harvest time I will tell the reapers, Gather the weeds first and bind them in bundles to be burned, but gather the wheat into my barn.' [Mt 13.24-30]

Making a human judgment is therefore by no means straightforward, even when it is necessary; other people may be adversely affected, and there must always be an awareness that the final arbiter is God himself. A later chapter in Matthew's Gospel offers guidance about the kind of process that might be appropriate in tackling human failings, which – despite the addition of the words *against you* in just a few manuscript sources – are not simply those that occur in personal disputes:

> If your brother sins (*against you*), go and tell him his fault, between you and him alone. If he listens to you, you have gained your brother. But if he does not listen, take one or two others along with you, that every word may be confirmed by the evidence of two or three witnesses. If he refuses to listen to them, tell it to the church; and if he refuses to listen even to the church, let him be to you as a Gentile and a tax collector. [Mt 18.15-17]

Discrimination is exercised here by the Christian community as a whole. If the offender remains unrepentant, it might seem that he is rejected outright – but that is not at all what the passage implies. 'Gentiles' and 'tax collectors', it should be recalled, were very much the focus of Christian outreach; hence, the loss# of 'sinners' never put them beyond the reach of the community's compassionate concern. Such were among 'the sheep', 'the coins', and 'the prodigal son' described in the parables of Luke 15.

There is a related passage in John's Gospel, although it is often mistranslated. The commission to Jesus' disciples occurs in chapter 20. In the Revised Standard Version it reads 'If you forgive the sins of any, they are forgiven; if you retain the sins of any, they are retained' [Jn 20.23]; but the repetition of 'sins' does not appear in the Greek original. It can be argued that in the immediate context it might be understood implicitly as the object of the verb 'retain'; but the wider context includes Jesus' own confession in his so-called 'High Priestly prayer' of John 17, which certainly suggests that verse 23 here should be compatible with it:

> While I was with them, I kept them in thy name, which thou hast given me; I have guarded them, and none of them is lost but the son of perdition, that the scripture might be fulfilled.

It is in the spirit of this teaching that the post-Easter injunction can be interpreted as 'If you forgive the sins of any, they are forgiven; if you retain (people), they (the Christian flock) are retained (rather than lost)'. The charge is a responsibility of care, to be exercised with prudence and with the same love that was in Christ: it is not the application of canon law, nor of inflexible rules, but a task requiring both wisdom and mercy – hence Jesus' bestowal of the Holy Spirit to provide divine guidance. In Luke's Gospel his comparable final words are 'that repentance and forgiveness of sins should be preached in his name to all nations, beginning from Jerusalem ... but stay in the city, until you are clothed with power from on high'.

The gift of the Holy Spirit, it should be remembered, was for the whole Church, for the body of believers and not just for those set apart through ordination. It was John Henry Newman's study of the Arian crisis in the 4th century that led him to comment on the human frailties that might sometimes affect even the most prestigious of Christian leaders. He wrote a controversial article *On Consulting the Faithful* in 1859 which put him under a shadow in Rome for several years afterwards:

> There were untrustworthy councils, unfaithful bishops, there was weakness, fear of consequences, misguidance, delusion, hallucination, endless, hopeless, extending itself into nearly every corner of the Catholic Church.

He pointed out that it was the Christian laity who then saved the day! Five years later, under attack in England from Charles Kingsley, who attributed to him words that indicated an unduly cavalier attitude to truthfulness among Catholic priests, Newman responded with his passionate self-defence, *Apologia Pro Vita Sua*. He explained that the search for truth was at the heart of his faith, but was not to be conceived as simplistically as Kingsley seemed to imagine:

> Catholic Christendom is no simple exhibition of religious absolutism, but presents a continuous picture of authority and private judgment alternately advancing and retreating as the ebb and flow of the tide.

Indeed, in one of his earlier sermons he had spoken in remarkably similar terms:

> We advance to the truth by experience of error; we succeed through failures. We know not how to do right except by having done wrong ... Such is the process by which we succeed; we walk to heaven backwards.

Those who dogmatically insist on a particular form of words or other such formulations of divine truth (which may indeed have been very necessary and helpful in one historical set of circumstances) tend to overlook the ineffable wonder and mystery of God's being. In the Jewish tradition his name was not even to be spoken. For Christians it is true that the Father has revealed himself in his incarnate Son; but even so, there are 'yet many things' into which little by little 'the Spirit of truth' will guide us [Jn 16.12-13]. The Letter to the Hebrews opens with the reminder that 'God spoke of old to our fathers' 'in many and various ways', and although it points to Jesus as the supreme exemplar of his message (his Word) we are still learning its full meaning and its 'many and various' implications. There is therefore a place within the Church for those who challenge previous interpretations in order to bring out aspects of the truth that may have been overlooked or neglected, or perhaps to give expression to God's purposes in more contemporary idioms. Likewise, we should appreciate that 'doubt' is not necessarily inimical to the Gospel: indeed, when we read of 'Doubting' Thomas, we acknowledge that he raised key questions not just for himself but on behalf of every later generation; and similarly, when at the end of Matthew's Gospel it is recorded that 'some' of the eleven disciples who saw Jesus alive on the Galilean mountain also 'doubted', it reassures us that the Easter experience was not a naïve fabrication or an hallucination but was subject to rigorous confirmation.

The richness of God's being

It is worth recalling that when, in the Old Testament, Moses encountered God in the burning bush and received his commission to lead the Israelites to freedom, he asked his name – what was he to say to the people? – and received the response 'I am who I am' [Exod 3.14].

The source of all being is thus beyond human words and definitions. In John's Gospel we are reminded of this truth in the language Jesus uses of himself – 'I am the way, the truth, and the life', 'I am the bread of life', 'I am the resurrection and the life', 'I am the good shepherd', 'I am the gate' – imagery which hints at the richness of his being and the variety of ways in which we can relate to him. No one metaphor is adequate, because no human situation is ever completely 'stereotypical': on our pilgrimage through life, changing circumstances may prompt us to look at times for support, or for guidance, or for encouragement; or maybe God challenges us in ways we have never previously considered. In words taken from Newman's famous prayer,

> God has created me to do Him some definite service. He has committed some work to me which He has not committed to another. I have my mission. I may never know it in this life, but I shall be told it in the next. I am a link in a chain, a bond of connection between persons. He has not created me for naught. I shall do good; I shall do His work.

Newman was always insistent that, as unique individuals, no two of us have quite the same calling. To use the phrase from Hebrews, we are 'many and various' – or in Newman's words 'people are variously constituted', so that 'what influences one does not influence another'. He added (in an article for *The Rambler*) 'I do not say that my way is better than another's; but it is my way, and an allowable way'.

To take but one of our Lord's 'I am' sayings: when he referred to himself as 'the gate', whereas one contemporary image that may spring to mind is the intimidating security barrier which allows us to pass only if our documents are in order and then to proceed only on a carefully demarcated route beyond, this is far from his intent. Again and again, the New Testament reminds us that the Christian life cannot be reduced to a code of requirements: this was why Jesus resisted the narrow legalism of the Pharisees. It is not the letter of the law that governs our response to the invitation of his grace, but the spirit that inflames us with the many Christian virtues. Paul suggests a few of them:

> Put on then, as God's chosen ones, holy and beloved, compassion, kindness, lowliness, meekness, and patience, forbearing one another and, if one has a complaint against another, forgiving each other; as the Lord has forgiven you, so you also must forgive. And above all these put on love, which binds everything together in perfect harmony. And let the peace of Christ rule in your hearts, to which indeed you were called in the one body. And be thankful. Let the word of Christ dwell in you richly, teach and admonish one another in all wisdom, and sing psalms and hymns and spiritual songs with thankfulness in your hearts to God. [Col 3.12-16]

It is worth exploring Jesus' gate imagery a little further. It takes us back to the story of mankind in the garden of Eden. Adam and Eve are in paradise, but they fall to temptation. They are not content with their lot, and (like us) are greedy for more – they want everything: where the Bible refers to 'the tree of the knowledge of good and evil', it uses a Hebrew idiom implying both good and evil and everything in between. The myth of our beginnings tells us that such desire is not only excessive, it is self-defeating. Adam and Eve are driven out of paradise:

> At the east of the garden of Eden God placed the cherubim, and a flaming sword which turned every way, to guard the way to the tree of life. [Gen 3.24]

In effect, therefore, in describing himself as 'the gate', Jesus is offering a way back. No barriers are proof against him, as his rising from the dead demonstrated definitively. His way of living can restore us to paradise once again, although it is not necessarily the obvious choice:

> Enter by the narrow gate; for the gate is wide and the way is easy, that leads to destruction, and those who enter by it are many. For the gate is narrow and the way is hard, that leads to life, and those who find it are few. [Mt 7.13-14]

The Greek word translated here as 'hard' derives from *thlipsis*, meaning 'tribulation', which has certainly been the experience of many Christians from the very first. Thus, when Paul and Barnabas travelled through what is present-day Turkey they strengthened

> the souls of the disciples, exhorting them to continue in the faith, and saying that through many *tribulations* we must enter the kingdom of God. [Acts 14.22]

This is entirely consistent with the recurrence in the New Testament of exhortations to be *patient* and to *persevere* – words high on the list for their frequency of use.

A related parable of our Lord is that of the seed, which although scattered liberally, too often fails to yield a rich harvest, being choked elsewhere by weeds or starved by the infertility of the soil. In all three Synoptic Gospels it is followed by the analogy of the 'mustard' seed, which, although the smallest of all seeds, grows into the greatest of shrubs. The point is not always grasped that this plant had no connection with mustard as we know it today, but was a weed – so easily taken to be worthless by those who lacked (spiritual) discernment. It tells us too that, although Jesus' gate is described as 'narrow' and his way tests those who find it, this is not because his mercy and grace are in poor supply nor that his Church is expected to have the narrowness of mind that seems to have characterized some of the Pharisees. On the contrary, Jesus commends his own generosity of spirit to Peter (forgive 'seventy times seven') and to all his disciples ('love your enemies, do good to those who hate you').

God's generosity is illustrated too in the Apocalypse in its concluding chapters. The return of paradise is likened to 'the holy city Jerusalem coming down out of heaven from God' [Apoc 21.10]. It has, not one, but twelve gates, which 'shall never be shut by day – and there shall be no night there' [Apoc 21.25]; 'the glory and the honour of the nations' will be gathered into the city. So, nothing that is good will be lost, and the implication is clear that – as Newman recognized – there are many 'allowable' options for Christ's followers, who may in the end enter the holy city through different gates. The number 'twelve' is of course symbolic of his chosen apostles, a very mixed bunch of men as were the twelve tribes of Israel whom they supplant. The tradition that they later diversified their mission across the globe to reach people of different languages and cultures is entirely consistent with Jesus' original intent:

> Go therefore and make disciples of all nations. [Mt 28.19]

Its fulfilment is glimpsed, according to Luke's account in Acts, on the day of Pentecost itself by those who were gathered in Jerusalem; each one heard the message in his or her 'own tongue'. John the Seer presents the same evangelistic challenge in his imagery of the river of life that waters whatever grows on its banks:

> On either side of the river, the tree of life with its twelve kinds of fruit, yielding its fruit each month; and the leaves of the tree were for the healing of the nations. [Rev 22.2]

Just as there is a plurality of canonical gospels, each bearing its particular witness to the person of our Lord, and a plurality of leaves and fruits, so we must respect the plurality of ways in which each of us walks in his footsteps – a plurality of callings, or in Paul's words, varieties of 'gifts', of 'service', and of 'working':

> To each is given the manifestation of the Spirit for the common good. [1 Cor 12.7]

The New Testament is abundantly clear that, although we encounter many a 'false' spirit – described by John as 'the spirit of antichrist' and 'the spirit of error' [1 Jn 4.3,6] – lurking to deceive us, the Holy Spirit remains alive and active. John also reminds us, in the conversation between Jesus and Nicodemus, that the Spirit can sometimes move us in unexpected directions: 'the wind blows where it wills ... you do not know whither it goes ... so it is with everyone who is born of the Spirit' [Jn 3.8]. Individual lives as well as the Church's mission need therefore to be ready for new callings which may well require different commitments and fresh forms of expression. A refocusing of resources is also sometimes necessary, especially (according to John 15) if there are 'branches' of Christ 'the vine' that bear little fruit and need pruning or – more drastically – being cut away altogether.

Examples of Christians responding creatively to circumstances can be seen in the apostolic age itself. Although baptism usually occurs in the presence of an established church community after appropriate instruction, the early chapters of Acts record Philip the evangelist spontaneously baptizing the Ethiopian eunuch in a pool by the roadside [8.26-40]; this is followed by Peter, soon after his arrival in Caesarea, declaring that those who had just spoken in tongues (the centurion Cornelius and his friends) should all be baptized [10.44-48]; in turn, Paul baptizes the gaoler from whose prison he has miraculously escaped shortly after the latter's conversion [Acts 16.22-34]. A new ministry had also developed in Jerusalem: to cope with rising numbers of disciples, and as a consequence the neglect of widows in the daily distribution, hands were laid on seven men, usually termed 'deacons', to relieve the Twelve of such practical responsibilities [Acts 6.1-16]. As Paul's ministry developed, he too was both innovative (as we have noted, in relation to the incorporation of the Gentiles) and flexible in planning his future work:

> They attempted to go into Bithynia, but the Spirit of Jesus did not allow them. [Acts 16.7]

> I hope to spend some time with you, if the Lord permits. But I will stay in Ephesus until Pentecost, for a wide door for effective work has opened to me. [1 Cor 16.7–9]

> When I came to Troas to preach the gospel of Christ, a door was opened for me in the Lord; but my mind could not rest because I did not find my brother Titus there. So I took leave of them and went on to Macedonia. [2 Cor 2.12–13]

> To me to live is Christ, and to die is gain. If it is to be life in the flesh, that means fruitful labour for me ... My desire is to depart and to be with Christ, for that is far better. But to remain in the flesh is more necessary on your account. [Phil 1.21–24]

In this last example, Paul sees his imprisonment, not as a setback, but as a witness to his guards and as an emboldening of the Christian community 'to speak the word of God without fear'. Luke presents the earlier persecution in Jerusalem [Acts 8.1] in the same light:

> Now those who were scattered went about preaching the word. [Acts 8.4]

The above passage from Philippians also marks a significant modification in Paul's thinking. No longer does he speak of death as a falling asleep, thence to be 'caught up in the clouds to meet the Lord in the air' [1 Thess 4.17 cf. 1 Cor 15.20]; nor is the prospect that of becoming 'alive' again at Christ's coming [1 Cor 15.22–23]. In this letter from prison, faced with his own possible demise, death is seen as a path taking him more fully 'to be with Christ'.

Thus, acting and thinking imaginatively under the guidance of the Holy Spirit is a normal part of Christian life. It is not always a popular option, and there are many examples of those who have been inhibited from doing so by authorities within the Church, or by overly conservative attitudes among both clergy and laity. A particularly shocking instance was the treatment of Mary Ward in the early 17th century. Her vocation was to found an order of women religious devoted to providing schooling for girls, and several houses were established across Europe. They were opposed on various grounds:

- Freedom from enclosure was not allowed by canon law for women's congregations.
- It constituted a constant danger for the moral life of its members.
- The consumption of their dowries placed any members who left in moral danger.
- The 'Jesuitesses' took a vow binding them to the instruction of girls and uneducated women, yet they lacked the permission of the local bishops.

Mary Ward's problem was that she refused to accept enclosure and wanted her Institute to be free to move around in the service of the wider Church under the direction of the Pope. In January 1631, the Papal Bull *Pastoralis Romani Pontificis* was issued, one of the harshest bulls ever written, declaring her to be a heretic and schismatic. The bull was read to her as she lay ill and she was led away to imprisonment at the Poor Clares convent in Munich. She remained there for nine weeks, where she was denied access to the sacraments, until Pope Urban relented. Whenever she met him, he was invariably kind, but in her absence, he succumbed to her enemies and destroyed her reputation. At heart, he could not understand that women might serve God in a similar way to men. In the end, however, she was able to return to England, and after her death her Institute was gradually re-established. Subsequently Pope Pius XII called her *'that incomparable woman whom Catholic England gave to the Church'*.

Steps that appear too innovative can thus prove remarkably divisive and may have to bide their time. We are nevertheless challenged, both as individuals and as a Church, to reflect on the question: how, in often rapidly changing times, does God want us now to witness to the generous, forgiving and creative love of Jesus himself? In what 'many and varied' ways should we express it today?

Here is testimony from a distant missionary region in northeastern India. I quote from an article by Monsignor John Kozar who visited the area not long ago:

> The greatest witness that happens is that they (the missionaries) live in the same conditions as the tribal people, inviting them to get to know them, to get to know how they pray … There is no presumption that anything will happen, but in these situations people draw closer to Jesus. They are learning stories about the faith … You're taking people who had no religious affiliation, but they have this yearning to relate to a higher power … Tribal languages are initially a barrier, but religious are making portions of the Bible available, and are beginning to train catechists. (However) the churches have to resist the temptation to build institutions. *This is about giving witness by living with the people.*

Britain today is also mission territory; yet, while the approach adopted in northeastern India may offer valuable insights, we also need to be open to what is culturally appropriate in our own situation and ready to 'hear what the Spirit says to the churches' [Rev 2.7,11,17,29; 3.6,13,22]. In past centuries there have been unanticipated developments which proved highly beneficial; thus, Christian mission has been enhanced (for example) by those serving alongside the clergy as monks or friars, or latterly by predominantly lay movements such as Focolare or L'Arche. Hans Urs von Balthasar once pointed out that historically God has often proved to be full of surprises, with new charisms coming 'like a bolt of lightning from the blue, destined to illuminate a single and original point of God's will for the Church in a given time'.

The following observation by Ian Ker writing about *The New Movements* is particularly germane in our own secularized circumstances:

> Where once it was enough to preach to people who still retained a substantial degree of belief in Christianity but whose practice of the faith was defective, in the contemporary world it is increasingly necessary to show people experientially that the gospel 'works', that is to say, that the love of Christ makes possible a new kind of happiness and hope. Missionaries to pagan countries have traditionally made their preaching 'incarnate' by means of hospitals and schools. But *in a secular society the gospel comes alive and real to people when it is 'incarnate' in a community context*. In other words, the gospel supplies a deeply felt need – the dreadful lack of community ... where(ever) people are forced to live highly individualistic, isolated lives **in an alienating environment.**

In the early Church there were few missionaries *per se* after the time of the apostles, and no missionary orders at all; but there were vibrant faith communities who won the hearts and minds of their contemporaries, and there were charismatic Christians who testified convincingly to the unfailing love of the Man for others. So, only a few decades ago, Pope John XXIII's prayer at the opening of the 2nd Vatican Council was for the dawning of a new Pentecost when once again 'the mighty works of God' would come alive and real for peoples across the world.

Jesus raises Adam and Eve
Fresco in Holy Saviour Church, Chora, Istanbul c. 1315

Jesus meets Mary Magdalen in the garden
Fra Angelico 1438

The disciples greet Jesus with their miraculous catch
Duccio c. 1300

Jesus has ascended
Ivory fragment from triptych early 9th century

5. His political challenge

The kingdom of God

Many of Jesus' parables speak of God's coming kingdom. This theme is embedded too in the prayer he gave us, which includes the familiar words 'Thy kingdom come, thy will be done, on earth as it is in heaven'. According to Mark, Jesus' opening proclamation included the message 'The kingdom of God is at hand'. Subsequently, when asked by the Pharisees when this kingdom was coming [Lk 17.21], his response was more carefully qualified:

> The kingdom of God is not coming with signs to be observed; nor will they say, 'Lo, here it is!' or 'There!' for behold, the kingdom of God is in the midst of you.

What he meant by these words is not entirely transparent, but it is likely that some of his contemporaries would have interpreted them as an indication that the long-awaited 'messianic reign' of peace and prosperity was imminent. Indeed, Jesus' disciples 'supposed that the kingdom of God was to appear immediately' [Lk 19.11]: by way of response, he told them the parable of the *mina* (a sum of money), which is about a nobleman who required his servants to use his gifts profitably as they awaited his return. The implication is therefore that, while the kingdom is beginning to break in, its plenitude requires more time and patience. Suffering too will be needed; at the Last Supper Jesus points to his own role in preparing the ground:

> I tell you that from now on I shall not drink of the fruit of the vine until the kingdom of God comes. [Lk 22.18]

Something of a polarity therefore emerges in the Gospels between such blessedness as may presently be experienced and its more glorious fulfilment that yet awaits. In several parables, such as 'the wheat and the tares', 'the labourers in the vineyard' or 'the sheep and the goats', there is a future denouement that clarifies – and perhaps confounds – our human assessment of God's rewards and those reckoned to be worthy of them. Indeed,

> How hard it will be for those who have riches to enter the kingdom of God. [Mk 10.23]

Put differently, the signs by which we judge are not necessarily those that count with God, who has some surprises in store for us. Yet for those who understand his purposes the kingdom is indeed 'at hand' – for example, in the receptiveness and simplicity of children, 'to such belongs the kingdom of God' [Mk 10.14]. Jesus can even quote a psalm that tells us so:

> Out of the mouths of babes and sucklings thou hast brought perfect praise. [Ps 8.1-2]

Again, there is the repentant thief, whose childlike yearning not to be forgotten in the coming kingdom is met with the Lord's promise that he would 'that very day' be with him in Paradise [Lk 23.43]. Many people would reckon him an unlikely candidate for such a reward, and might well be shocked by the generosity of Jesus' offer. But elsewhere we have a parabolic explanation:

> And he said, "With what can we compare the kingdom of God, or what parable shall we use for it? It is like a grain of mustard seed, which, when sown upon the ground, is the smallest of all the seeds on earth; yet when it is sown it grows up and becomes the greatest of all shrubs, and puts forth large branches, so that the birds of the air can make nests in its shade. [Mk 4.30-32]

In the Palestinian context, as noted above, 'mustard' was all but a weed. So Jesus is turning our conventional attitudes on their head – in God's kingdom some who 'are last will be first', and vice versa [Lk 13.28-30]

In plainer terms Jesus rejected worldly views of 'the kingdom':

> Again, the devil took him to a very high mountain, and showed him all the kingdoms of the world and the glory of them; and he said to him, "All these I will give you, if you will fall down and worship me." Then Jesus said to him, "Begone, Satan! for it is written, 'You shall worship the Lord your God and him only shall you serve. [Mt 4.8-10]

If that *pericope* summarized the kind of internal debate which Jesus needed to resolve before commencing his ministry, he certainly never wavered from this position thereafter. He taught his disciples to 'seek first (God's) kingdom' [Mt 6.33] – any other necessities of life would be theirs as well (with the unspoken proviso that God is the best judge of such requirements, not they themselves). Then, in one of Jesus' final clashes, he faced Pontius Pilate in person:

> Jesus answered, "My kingship is not of this world; if my kingship were of this world, my servants would fight, that I might not be handed over to the Jews; but my kingship is not from the world." Pilate said to him, "So you are a king?" Jesus answered, "You say that I am a king. For this I was born, and for this I have come into the world, to bear witness to the truth. Everyone who is of the truth hears my voice. [Jn 18.36-37]

Christians live therefore in a state of tension between two worlds: there is the existing ordering of life on earth, and there is the divine intention for human affairs, which commands our more fundamental loyalty. God is 'king' in our lives when we do his will – as is clearly indicated in the Lord's Prayer ('thy kingdom come, they will be done on earth as it is in heaven'). But as Jesus pointed out,

> No one can serve two masters; for either he will hate the one and love the other, or he will be devoted to the one and despise the other. You cannot serve God and mammon. [Mt 6.24; Lk 16.13]

This certainly requires Christians to clarify their priorities, and there are a number of gospel passages which reflect on the choices to be made; for example, God's kingdom is likened to buried treasure, or again to the 'one pearl of great value' for which everything else may be readily sacrificed. It is not necessarily a stark opposition of 'good' versus 'evil', but may often be more of a search for what is 'best'. Paul so urged the Christians in Philippi:

> Finally, brethren, whatever is true, whatever is honorable, whatever is just, whatever is pure, whatever is lovely, whatever is gracious, if there is any excellence, if there is anything worthy of praise, think about these things. [Phil 4.8]

Nevertheless, situations and their attendant issues are likely to arise where loyalties can be severely strained:

> They sent to (Jesus) some of the Pharisees and some of the Herodians, to entrap him in his talk. And they came and said to him,

> "Teacher, we know that you are true, and care for no man; for you do not regard the position of men, but truly teach the way of God. Is it lawful to pay taxes to Caesar, or not? Should we pay them, or should we not?" But knowing their hypocrisy, he said to them, "Why put me to the test? Bring me a coin, and let me look at it." And they brought one. And he said to them, "Whose likeness and inscription is this?" They said to him, "Caesar's." Jesus said to them, "Render to Caesar the things that are Caesar's, and to God the things that are God's." And they were amazed at him. [Mk 12.13-17]

In the earliest Christian decades this was undoubtedly the stance promoted by the apostles and their successors. Paul himself was not ashamed of his Roman citizenship, and when on trial in Jerusalem made reference to it in order to gain a fair hearing for himself [Acts 21.39], in the end appealing to Caesar himself [Acts 25.8-12], 'though I had no charge to bring against my nation' [Acts 28.19]. There are of course various references to Roman commanders and officials who were won over by Jesus himself or by the early Church. Luke's two volume work is addressed to the 'most excellent Theophilus', partly motivated by the desire to remove any lurking suspicion in his mind that Christians could be seditious or that their faith was likely to be politically threatening. The 1st Letter to Timothy sets out what appears to be clear guidance:

> First of all, then, I urge that supplications, prayers, intercessions, and thanksgivings be made for all men, for kings and all who are in high positions, that we may lead a quiet and peaceable life, godly and respectful in every way. [1 Tim 2.1-2]

Yet offering prayer for civic authorities does not necessarily result in the desired response. As the 1st century progressed, it became evident that there were issues on which church and state could not agree, particularly those which involved forms of 'idolatrous' worship. Consciences were certainly troubled in Paul's time over 'food offered to idols' [1 Cor 8.1ff], but matters really came to a head over the imperial cult (in which the Roman emperor was held to be divine). One of the latest writings in the New Testament reminds us that Christians were for several centuries sporadically persecuted:

> I John, your brother, who share with you in Jesus the tribulation and the kingdom and the patient endurance, was on the island called

Patmos on account of the word of God and the testimony of Jesus. [Apoc 1.9]

The secular power is now described as 'the beast', or as a 'harlot'; Rome is not named as such, but is likened to Babylon, Israel's great enemy of bygone centuries. Although it may seem to retain the upper hand, Christians are urged to take heart. The beast and his allied subjects

> will make war on the Lamb, and the Lamb will conquer them, for he is Lord of lords and King of kings, and those with him are called and chosen and faithful. [Apoc 17.14]

Rome's false ideology has led to its fatal corruption, and hence its eventual downfall:

> Fallen, fallen is Babylon the great! It has become a dwelling place of demons, a haunt of every foul spirit, a haunt of every foul and hateful bird; for all nations have drunk the wine of her impure passion, and the kings of the earth have committed fornication with her, and the merchants of the earth have grown rich with the wealth of her wantonness. [Apoc 18.2-3]

There is a limit, therefore, beyond which Christians have to renounce their secular allegiances. Paul exhorted his Roman readers not to be 'conformed to this world, but be transformed by the renewal of your mind' [Rom 12.2]. In the words of Peter and the apostles, when resisting the temple authorities of Jerusalem,

> We must obey God rather than men. [Acts 5.29]

Or, as the Letter to the Hebrews (probably written in Rome in the late 1st century) urged with enhanced theological justification:

> Jesus suffered outside the gate in order to sanctify the people through his own blood. Therefore, let us go forth to him outside the camp and bear the abuse he endured. For here we have no lasting city, but we seek the city which is to come. [Heb 13.12-13]

A 2nd century apologetic writing, the *Letter to Diognetus*, includes a famous passage which expands this teaching:

> Christians are indistinguishable from other men either by nationality, language or customs. They do not inhabit separate cities of their own, or speak a strange dialect, or follow some outlandish way of

life. Their teaching is not based upon reveries inspired by the curiosity of men. Unlike some other people, they champion no purely human doctrine. With regard to dress, food and manner of life in general, they follow the customs of whatever city they happen to be living in, whether it is Greek or foreign.

And yet there is something extraordinary about their lives. They live in their own countries as though they were only passing through. They play their full role as citizens, but labour under all the disabilities of aliens. Any country can be their homeland, but for them their homeland, wherever it may be, is a foreign country. Like others, they marry and have children, but they do not expose them. They share their meals, but not their wives.

They live in the flesh, but they are not governed by the desires of the flesh. They pass their days upon earth, but they are citizens of heaven. Obedient to the laws, they yet live on a level that transcends the law. Christians love all men, but all men persecute them. Condemned because they are not understood, they are put to death, but raised to life again. They live in poverty, but enrich many; they are totally destitute, but possess an abundance of everything. They suffer dishonour, but that is their glory. They are defamed, but vindicated. A blessing is their answer to abuse, deference their response to insult. For the good they do they receive the punishment of malefactors, but even then they, rejoice, as though receiving the gift of life. They are attacked by the Jews as aliens, they are persecuted by the Greeks, yet no one can explain the reason for this hatred.

To speak in general terms, we may say that the Christian is to the world what the soul is to the body. As the soul is present in every part of the body, while remaining distinct from it, so Christians are found in all the cities of the world, but cannot be identified with the world. As the visible body contains the invisible soul, so Christians are seen living in the world, but their religious life remains unseen.

A later document known as the *Apostolic Tradition*, which dates mainly from the following century, is rather more guarded and expresses certain qualifications about what was expected of catechumens in Rome. It is clear that some occupations and associated practices were incompatible with Christianity:

Inquiry shall be made about the professions and trades of those who are brought to be admitted to the faith. If a man is a pander, he must desist or be rejected. If a man is a sculptor or painter, he must be charged not to make idols; if he does not desist he must be rejected. If a man is an actor or pantomimist, he must desist or be rejected. A teacher of young children had best desist, but if he has no other occupation, he may be permitted to continue. A charioteer, likewise, who races or frequents races, must desist or be rejected. A gladiator or a trainer of gladiators, or a huntsman (in the wild beast shows), or anyone connected with these shows, or a public official in charge of gladiatorial exhibitions must desist or be rejected. A heathen priest or anyone who tends idols must desist or be rejected. A soldier of the civil authority must be taught not to kill men and to refuse to do so if he is commanded, and to refuse to take an oath; if he is unwilling to comply, he must be rejected. A military commander or civic magistrate that wears the purple must resign or be rejected. If a catechumen or a believer seeks to become a soldier, they must be rejected, for they have despised God. A harlot or licentious man or one who has castrated himself, or any other who does things not to be named, must be rejected, for they are defiled. A magician must not (even) be brought for examination. An enchanter, an astrologer, a diviner, a soothsayer, a user of magic verses, a juggler, a mountebank, an amulet-maker must desist or be rejected. [*Ap Trad* 16]

Individual Christian writers of much the same period also express disapproval of such occupations, and of others besides – thus, Clement of Alexandria viewed perfumers in particular as 'frivolous'. But Christians were not alone: the Jewish *Talmud* thought ass-drivers, barbers, sailors and shopkeepers were beyond the pale. Such principled engagement with a secular society might of course result in some being unemployed, but that was the price to be paid by a developed conscience.

A good deal of this changed in the fourth century, following the emperor Constantine's conversion. It meant that the Church was no longer a predominantly lower class, somewhat despised, minority who revered their martyrs; Christians were now accepted into the imperial mainstream, and some even held important public roles. The dynamics of combining everyday living while yet preparing to dwell in the heavenly realm therefore underwent significant revision. At one level there was greater tolerance of practices that might still be regarded with some disfavour: the rationale for this might be described as 'gradualism', which allowed that it would take time for many who converted to the Christian faith to adjust to its distinctive ethos.

A more urgent need was to modify the predominantly pacifist tradition that stemmed from Christ's teaching on 'turning the other cheek', given the weight of responsibility for state security that now rested partly on Christian shoulders. It had already begun to be recognized that the personal challenge 'to return good for evil' must be weighed alongside the need to protect the weak and helpless. There are certainly earlier instances of Christians performing military service; but it was in the 380s that Ambrose of Milan turned not only to the Bible for guidance on the vexed subject, but to the distinguished Latin writer Cicero. By now there were a number of 'pagan' authors (for example, Plato as well as Cicero) who were credited with at least some degree of divine guidance, and were therefore worthy of Christian attention. Much of Ambrose's social thought expressed in his *De Officiis* ('On Duties') was thus informed by ideas gleaned from Cicero, although the biblical emphasis was certainly his own.

What mattered most to him was the co-responsibility Christians held for one another, whether rich or poor – their mutual solidarity:

> Good will is now enhanced by the communal nature of the church, by our partnership in faith, by our kinship as recipients of the grace of baptism, and by our sharing in the Mysteries ... By these means the congregation of the holy church grows ever upwards into one body, joined and bound together in the unity of faith and love.

Nor was it only faith and love that rich and poor were called to share: a greater pooling of earthly wealth was also implied.

> God has ordained all things to be produced so that there should be food in common for all and that the earth should be the common possession of all. Nature has produced a common right for all, but greed has made it a right for the few.

It might well be necessary too for the strong to be called upon sometimes in defence of the weak; not so doing might be a failure of neighbourly love. By extension, the use of force to protect a nation might on occasion be justified. Here, once again, Ambrose was able to draw upon Cicero, who argued that war is to be waged only in the pursuit of attaining peace; that it should spare non-combatants and be merciful to those who surrender; that it is only soldiers under oath of service who may legitimately fight; that the humanity of one's enemy must be recognized, imposing restrictions therefore upon the conduct of war; that any agreements made should be honoured; and that no unfair advantage should be taken of the enemy. Yet Ambrose's presentation was thoroughly biblical. We can observe, for example, a provocative core already existing in John the Baptist's exhortations, which were implicitly endorsed by Jesus:

> And the multitudes asked him, "What then shall we do?" And he answered them, "He who has two coats, let him share with him who has none; and he who has food, let him do likewise." Tax collectors also came to be baptized, and said to him, "Teacher, what shall we do?" And he said to them, "Collect no more than is appointed you." Soldiers also asked him, "And we, what shall we do?" And he said to them, "Rob no one by violence or by false accusation, and be content with your wages". [Lk 3.10-14]

Although Ambrose made significant inroads into the Church's predominantly pacifist tradition, he left unresolved the issue of marrying the necessary external use of restraint with the Christian's calling to an inner disposition of love. There is no easy resolution, and the tension often manifests itself in individual combatants in what came to be termed 'shell shock' in the aftermath of the First World War. Psychoanalysts at the time began to understand that this was not simply a mental disturbance induced by the relentless noise of exploding artillery, but more profoundly a spiritual recoil from bestial behaviour (in Siegfried Sassoon's words, war is an 'outraging' of humanity).

Ambrose's greatest achievement, however, was to present the living and caring Church, not as a persecuted minority of true believers, but as the growing nucleus of God's true humanity. The implication was that any tension between the loyalties owed on the one hand to God and on the other to Caesar would best be resolved if the *mores* of God's kingdom were accepted universally.

Today's pressing issues

In the largely post-Christian world where many Western nations now find themselves, it is clear that we are once again in a much different situation. New ways of thinking, and new ideologies, continue to emerge; some have absorbed the Christian ethos, but others are inimical to it. It was nearly one hundred years ago (unsurprisingly in the aftermath of a hugely wasteful and destructive war) that the Catholic Church saw the dangerous rise of both communism and fascism. In response, the new Feast of Christ the King was instituted by Pius XI in 1925 as a direct appeal to young people not to be wooed by false promises. Here are some extracts from a sermon preached by Ronald Knox some years later.

> Christendom has before now taken up arms in its own defence; or even in a pathetic attempt to recover the Holy Places. Christian princes, before now, have tried to spread the faith at the point of the sword, always, or nearly always, with disastrous results for religion. But the substantial victories of the Church have lain, always, in the sphere of the human conscience. Christ has reigned, not in the councils of nations, but in men's hearts. If every country in the world professed the Catholic religion, set up religious emblems in its market places and voted special honours, special privileges, special revenues to the clergy—that would not be the reign of Christ on earth. It would not be the reign of Christ on earth if the homage which men paid to religion was merely external, merely political; if they treated the emblems of Christianity merely as an ancestral tradition they were proud of, and a convenient rallying-point for civic sentiment, no more. Christ will reign in the world only where, only in so far as, he rules in human hearts ...
>
> In the course of (Pius XI's) career he had seen more than it is given to most Popes to see. His background was a background of European culture; and circumstances had suddenly thrust under his eyes, after his sixtieth year, vivid impressions of that struggle between two great forces in Europe, nationalism and international socialism, which the rest of the world hardly suspected as yet. When he was crowned Pope (in 1922), he insisted on giving his blessing to the world from the balcony of St Peter's, a thing no Pope had done since the loss of the temporal power. Even so early, he had made up his mind that the Papacy must come out of its retirement, and make itself felt as a

moral force in the world. And I think he introduced this feast of the Kingship of Christ with the same idea in view. He saw that the minds of men, of young men especially, all over Europe, would be caught by a wave of conflicting loyalties, which would drown the voice of conscience, and produce everywhere unscrupulous wars between class and class, and the threat of equally unscrupulous wars between nations. To save the world, if he could, from that frenzy of reckless idealism, he would recall it to the contemplation of a very simple truth. The truth, I mean, that the claim of Christ comes first, before the claims of party, before the claims of nationality. *Pax Christi in regno Christi*; peace and justice were duties which man owed to God more elementary than any duties to his fellow men. All that, before the conflict between the Church and Fascism, before the revolution in Spain, before the name of Hitler had ever been set up in the type-room of a foreign newspaper. The institution of this feast was not a gesture of clericalism against anticlericalism, still less a gesture of authoritarianism against democracy. It was a gesture of Christian truth against a world which was on the point of going mad with political propaganda.

It affects us, you say, very little? True, we have seen little in our own country [Britain] of political violence; and probably we are on the whole less caught by political loyalties than any other nation in. the world. But we do not know what a day or an hour may bring forth. It may yet be important for men to be reminded in England, in our lifetime, that the claim of the divine law upon the human conscience comes before anything else.

Today there are different challenges and different slogans in the air. Communism is no longer a threat, but in its place is a rampant *individualism*, often linked to *consumerism* and *hedonism*. Fascism, however, has taken on a new guise in the form of multi-faceted *racism*. *Tribalism*, although usually associated with primal cultures in Africa and Asia, has never disappeared from Britain itself, albeit impacting more subtly through cultural and political discrimination. Its underlying *exclusivism* manifests itself too in the upsurge of *nationalism* across the world. In some countries there is a growing readiness to tolerate less familiar life-styles, but this derives more from an insistence upon individual freedom of expression than from any desire for mutual support and exchange within society. Likewise, global awareness remains weak, as does the appreciation of our (often disastrous) colonial and economic legacy: as the former Archbishop of Canterbury, Rowan Williams, once suggested in an interview,

> The major problems of the world are transnational and we are all locked into each other's fate more intensively than we were one hundred years ago ... the commitment to invest in the growing wellbeing of vulnerable societies is actually one of the most rational and constructive things we can do for ourselves.

It is not the task of the Church to propose detailed legislation for this or for any society; that is what might be termed Caesar's responsibility, but – again in Rowan Williams' recommendation –

> The Church is obliged to be both a good and an awkward neighbour to the state. It earns its place in a plural state by asking certain unwelcome questions.

Today, for example, the 'plural state' has sought to discover its own cohesiveness in what are commonly described as 'British values'. The official list, as taught to school children, now covers *democracy; the rule of law; individual liberty; mutual respect for and tolerance of those with different faiths and beliefs and for those without faith*. Unfortunately, these are rather vague notions, whose interpretation can vary enormously. 'Democracy' might, for example, mean 'a striving for consensus' – or it could simply mean the rule of the majority, who trample upon the rights of minorities. 'The rule of law' might be taken to refer solely to the resolution of disputes, and not to the obligation to observe a moral code of behaviour (thus allowing public figures who have acted shabbily to 'deny any wrong doing'). 'Individual liberty' is too much of an open invitation to pursue one's own interests without regard to the consequences (for example, becoming so alcohol- or drug-dependent that much public money is needed for aftercare). 'Mutual respect' does not necessarily extend to 'social inclusion' (as a Catholic priest I am well aware that heads of many schools would not countenance any contribution I might be able to make for the benefit of their children).

It is far more important to strive for *universal human values* than to discover any supposed Britishness that is currently fashionable in political circles. The above educational list might, for example, be altered to promote instead values such as *the common good; honesty; courtesy; and hospitality.* Alternative values suggested recently – namely, 'cohesion, courage and stability' – are surely 'weasel' words, capable of bearing any meaning that might be read into them, which Christians in a 'post-truth' society need to avoid. In an article in *The Tablet* the journalist Matthew d'Ancona suggested:

> Post-truth is not, as is sometimes assumed, just a newly fashionable description of lies, spin or disinformation. It describes a more complex phenomenon, in which emotional resonance is becoming more important than facts and evidence, and verification is being replaced by social media algorithms that tell us what we want to hear.

There are certainly facts and issues that today's Church needs to bring resolutely before the general public. Whereas a discussion of national 'cohesion' seems more likely to result in unresolved waffle, the plight of a beleaguered world in which thirty million are forced to leave their homes every year because of conflict, violence and natural disasters ought to dominate our political life as much as the state of the National Health Service. Likewise, our preoccupation with 'progress' (which supposedly improves our quality of life) ought to be seriously challenged by Christian thinkers: does it enhance life for all, or only for the few? does it demand a commercial infrastructure which traps many low-paid workers in jobs unworthy of their human dignity? does it encourage the vitality of the natural world on which we depend? does it indeed make us any happier? Again, why do we allow a significant part of our economy to depend upon arms exports that inevitably contribute to the world's instability? why is so much spent upon nuclear defences, given the many urgent needs that as a consequence go neglected?

At the personal level, there must surely be far more consideration given to the widespread availability of abusive and degrading material on the internet. The addictive use of smartphones and the impact of social media, particularly on young people, has reached alarming proportions: one outcome is the rapid increase in mental health problems, including rising rates of suicide and self-harm: arguably, it also diminishes the readiness of people to engage in face-to-face exchanges and limits the quality of any attention to their immediate environment. Aldous Huxley once warned that Orwellian-style coercion was less of a threat to democracy than the subtler power of psychological manipulation, and 'man's almost infinite appetite for distractions': the latter is equally a threat to family and community life. At the same time, it has long been evident that extreme political and religious ideas propagated so easily through the worldwide web have facilitated the formation of jihadist cells and have enabled terrorist activities to flourish in regions far removed from major centres of conflict such as the Middle East. These will no doubt increasingly include major cyber-attacks, which opens the question of how far we should be entrusting ourselves to ever more sophisticated computerised systems (and perhaps lives that are ruled by algorithms and robots?).

It is worth recalling that as thinkers in ancient times reflected upon present predicaments in the light of past history they came to lay great weight upon the virtue of wisdom, which certainly embraced the idea of 'far-sightedness': is it unfair to suggest that *short-termism* prevails too much today in political decision making? and that faith in technology is in danger of dehumanising the world? Jesus once commented,

> If a blind man leads a blind man, both will fall into a pit. [Mt 15.14]

These are but a sample of many more long-term issues, some of which have been helpfully addressed by papal encyclicals in recent decades. Perhaps the greatest political challenge that arises today from our Lord's life and ministry is to widen our vision, and to look beyond narrow self-interest (expressed, for example, in the promotion of lifestyles that impact harmfully upon others, as well as in the erection of ever more obstacles and barriers to keep the 'others' out of our way) in order to discover God's dream of a new world made in his image. The early Church cared very much to walk in step with Jesus; should we not look to their example and be more radical in our faith? There are so many people crying out for help in today's world: Christians should be among those who are listening to them, and in the forefront of those engaging with their plight. It may threaten our own well-being and prosperity to do so, but God's heart is surely generous enough to sustain us all.

The suffering body of Christ
St Addai, Iraq 2017

Christ's gathered body
Magomero, Malawi 2003

Christ's missionary outreach
DR Congo 2016

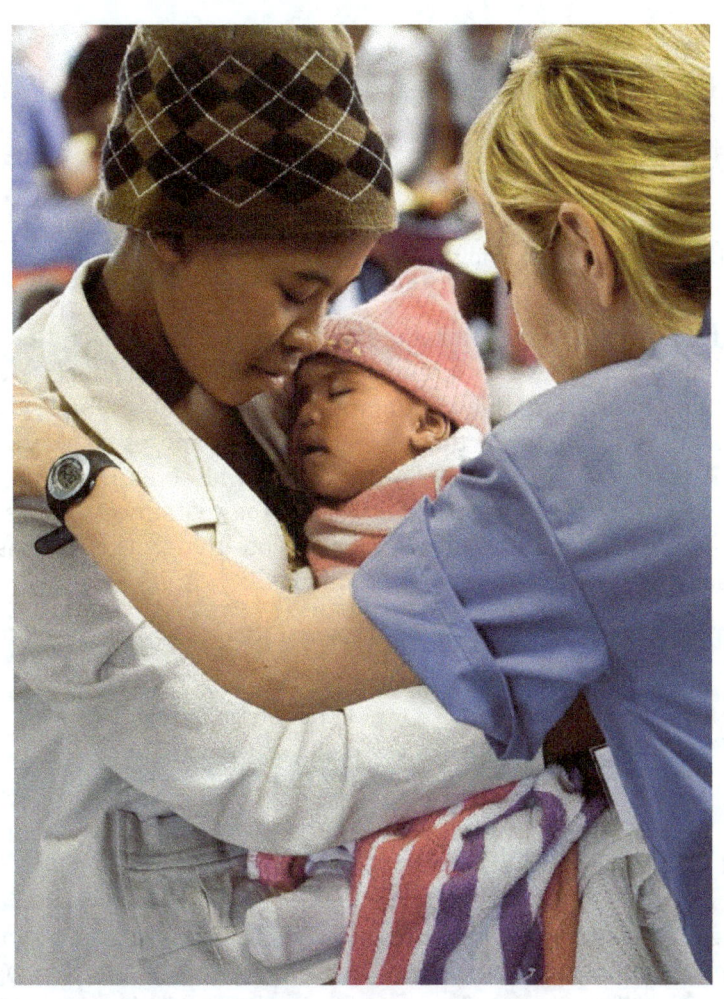

The caring body of Christ
South Africa 2015

6. His message

The time is fulfilled

The earliest Gospel known to us is that of St Mark, and the first words spoken by Jesus that he records are these:

> The time is fulfilled, and the kingdom of God is at hand; repent, and believe in the gospel. [Mk 1.15]

It is at once a challenging message, but also one of hope and promise. Repentance is urged, God's intentions for mankind having been thwarted by the ambitions of earthly kingdoms and the false imaginings of human hearts. In years gone by there were indeed glimpses of where true fulfilment might be found: alongside a widespread instinct that mankind's destiny was governed by higher spiritual powers, there were prophetic revelations that helped to articulate the proper responses to be made and the right paths to be trodden.

The most profound expression of our status occurs in the opening chapter of Genesis:

> Then God said, "Let us make man in our image, after our likeness". [Gen 1.26]

Much debate has taken place as to what human feature best reflects this divine 'likeness': since it is plainly not our *bodily* form, could it rather be found in some *mental* agility such as rationality or creativity, or should we look rather to potential *moral* or *spiritual* qualities? When St Bernard (in the 12th century) pondered this question, he turned it around: he pointed out that we cannot have any conception of God's 'image' in ourselves until we have a clearer understanding of God – for, as St Paul more than once quoted from Isaiah, 'who has known the mind of the Lord or who has been his counsellor' [Rom 11.34 cf 1 Cor 2.16, Isa 40.13]? Bernard continued:

> God was completely invisible and beyond our intellect – but now he wished to be comprehended, to be seen, to be pondered. But how? you may ask. I answer: lying in a manger, resting on a virgin's bosom, preaching on the mount, spending the night in prayer; or hanging on the cross, the pallor of death on his face, like one forsaken among the

dead, overruling the powers of hell; or rising again on the third day, showing the apostles the print of the nails, the sign of victory, and finally ascending from their sight into heaven ... If I reflect on any of these things, I reflect on God, and in all of them I find my God.

It is fitting, therefore, that the next words of Jesus in Mark's Gospel are addressed to his first disciples, Simon and Andrew:

> Follow *me* and I will make you become fishers of men. [Mk 1.17]

It is as Jesus' disciples that we can come to reflect the true 'image and likeness' of God, and in turn help others to discover the deeper meaning and fulfilment of their lives. Our own salvation therefore has an inclusive dimension – we, like our Lord, are called to be men and women 'for others'. We need to appreciate that our personal well-being is incomplete until God's kingdom has *fully* manifested itself; and in a world that increasingly stresses the individual, it should never be forgotten that God's revelation of himself as trinitarian means that we only reflect his image when our lives too are abundantly relational. There is indeed a common African saying which expresses our necessarily corporate existence: in Zulu, *umuntu ngumuntu nagabantu* – 'a person is a person because of other people', although for Christians this has a significantly more universal interpretation than the tribalism it too often expresses. Again, in the words of St Paul,

> We, though many, are one body in Christ, and individually members one of another. [Rom 12.5]

It is noticeable that in John's Gospel, Jesus' call of his first disciples is described a little differently from that of Mark:

> One of the two who heard John speak, and followed him, was Andrew, Simon Peter's brother.
> *He first found his brother Simon*, and said to him, "We have found the Messiah" (which means Christ). He brought him to Jesus. Jesus looked at him, and said, "So you are Simon the son of John? You shall be called Cephas" (which means Peter). The next day Jesus decided to go to Galilee. And he found Philip and said to him, "Follow me." Now Philip was from Bethsaida, the city of Andrew and Peter. *Philip found Nathanael*, and said to him, "We have found him of whom

> Moses in the law and also the prophets wrote, Jesus of Nazareth, the son of Joseph." [Jn 1.40-45]

So Andrew's immediate response to his own calling is to find his brother Simon; likewise, Philip goes at once in search of Nathanael. We later discover that, despite initial doubts about Jesus by his own brothers [Jn 7.5], before Pentecost has been reached they have been won over and have joined the disciples at prayer in the Upper Room in Jerusalem [Acts 1.14]. One of them, James, is seen years later as the leader of the Jerusalem church [Acts 15.13ff]. Whereas they had at first urged Jesus to show 'himself' (in messianic mode) to the world, they now accepted that his mission was to make God more fully known [Jn 1.18; 3.12; 5.19; 6.46 etc – in contrast to Jn 7.4].

Those familiar with the Hebrew scriptures may recall at this point that brothers were not always represented as so much in harmony or concerned with one another's welfare:

> Cain said to Abel his brother, "Let us go out to the field." And when they were in the field, Cain rose up against his brother Abel, and killed him. Then the Lord said to Cain, "Where is Abel your brother?" He said, "I do not know; am I my brother's keeper?"

Similar rivalry can be seen in subsequent narratives; for example, between Jacob and Esau, Joseph and his brothers, Jotham and Abimelech, Absalom and Amnon. Such clashes are familiar from folklore tales that often depict the youngest member of a family as the true hero, in contrast to his or her despicable older siblings – a worldview that highlights the opposition between good and evil.

Despite several of Jesus' parables that seem to reflect this stark polarity, on a closer reading we find that they are much more nuanced, allowing for responses (like those of his own brothers) to change and hopefully to mature over time. Here are a few examples:

- "What do you think? A man had two sons; and he went to the first and said, 'Son, go and work in the vineyard today.' And he answered, 'I will not'; but afterward he repented and went. And he went to the second and said the same; and he answered, 'I go, sir,' but did not go. Which of the two did the will of his father?" They said, "The first." Jesus said to them, "Truly, I say to you, the tax collectors and the harlots go into the kingdom of God before you. For John came to you in the way of righteousness, and you did not believe him, but the tax collectors and the harlots believed him; and even when you saw it, you did not afterward repent and believe him." [Mt 21.28-32]

- And he said, "There was a man who had two sons; and the younger of them said to his father, 'Father, give me the share of property that falls to me.' And he divided his living between them. Not many days later, the younger son gathered all he had and took his journey into a far country, and there he squandered his property in loose living. And when he had spent everything, a great famine arose in that country, and he began to be in want. So he went and joined himself to one of the citizens of that country, who sent him into his fields to feed swine. And he would gladly have fed on the pods that the swine ate; and no one gave him anything. But when he came to himself he said, 'How many of my father's hired servants have bread enough and to spare, but I perish here with hunger! I will arise and go to my father, and I will say to him, "Father, I have sinned against heaven and before you; I am no longer worthy to be called your son; treat me as one of your hired servants."' And he arose and came to his father. But while he was yet at a distance, his father saw him and had compassion, and ran and embraced him and kissed him. And the son said to him, 'Father, I have sinned against heaven and before you; I am no longer worthy to be called your son.' But the father said to his servants, 'Bring quickly the best robe, and put it on him; and put a ring on his hand, and shoes on his feet; and bring the fatted calf and kill it, and let us eat and make merry; for this my son was dead, and is alive again; he was lost, and is found.' And they began to make merry. Now his elder son was in the field; and as he came and drew near to the house, he heard music and dancing. And he called one of the servants and asked what this meant. And he said to him, 'Your brother has come, and your father has killed the fatted calf, because he has received him safe and sound.' But he was angry and refused to go in. His father came out and entreated him, but he answered his father, 'Lo, these many years I have served you, and I never disobeyed your command; yet you never gave me a kid, that I might make merry with my friends. But when this son of yours came, who has devoured your living with harlots, you killed for him the fatted calf!' And he said to him, 'Son, you are always with me, and all that is mine is yours. It was fitting to make merry and be glad, for this your brother was dead, and is alive; he was lost, and is found.'" [Lk 15.11-32]

- Two men went up into the temple to pray, one a Pharisee and the other a tax collector. The Pharisee stood and prayed thus with himself, 'God, I thank thee that I am not like other men, extortioners, unjust, adulterers, or even like this tax collector. I fast twice a week, I give tithes of all that I get.' But the tax collector, standing far off, would not even lift up his eyes to heaven, but beat his breast, saying, 'God, be merciful to me a sinner!' I tell you, that this man went down to his house justified rather than the other. [Lk 18.10-14]

Each of these parables has a surprise in store for us. The pattern is similar – we are introduced to a pair of characters whom we are initially tempted to classify in black and white terms: one seems to stand out as the more reliable and commendable person, the other being portrayed as the very opposite. Jesus, however, invites us to listen to their individual stories, and to observe how first impressions can be quite misleading. The less likely character in each case is the one who is open to change. Different factors have prompted reflection and deeper self-awareness: in the first story, the 'unwilling' son may have recalled how much his father had done for him in the past, and recognises that he now needs his help in return; the 'prodigal son' more straightforwardly has had to learn by his foolish mistakes; and as for the tax collector, his conscience has taken him to stand before God in the temple, whose forgiveness he needs more urgently than any wealth that may come his way. This 'openness to change' is key to the spirituality that Jesus wanted to promote: the Greek word used in the New Testament is *metanoia*, which translates literally as 'a change of mind'. Jesus' gospel is an invitation to adapt the Father's values and priorities, and to attune one's own heart to his heart.

Inevitably this is a process that takes time, so in the above parables we see only the beginning and the middle of each story: the 'ending' lies beyond us. This applies equally to the fate of both characters, the Pharisee as much as the tax collector, the older brother as well as his reformed sibling. Another parable that Jesus told makes this point very clearly – 'the wheat and the tares' as it has commonly been known. Jesus warned against the danger of hasty or premature action: 'in gathering the weeds', he pointed out, the wheat might be rooted up as well; hence they should be allowed to 'grown together until the harvest'. The analogy he drew would surely have been appreciated in what was then a predominantly rural society.

Jesus was ready to allow for reformation in people's lives; he was aware that bad habits and unhelpful attitudes can be overcome, that past mistakes can be redeemed, that the stereotyping of people as worthless sinners may well overlook the potential for goodness lying within them; and that 'what is impossible with men is possible with God' [Lk 18.27]. His warning is amplified elsewhere:

> Why do you see the speck that is in your brother's eye, but do not notice the log that is in your own eye? [Mt 7.3]

Jesus himself often offended the religious establishment of his day by defying customary expectations. He ate and drank with those whom the scribes dismissed as sinners; his disciples at times failed to maintain their ritual cleanliness before a meal; they also broke Sabbath rules (and so on). His explanation was simple: too much weight had been laid on 'the tradition of men', so that in effect God's word was made void through human teachings [Mk 7.1-13]. His emphasis lay upon God's own purposes of goodness and love: thus, he refused to categorize people simplistically as either 'the godly' or 'the ungodly', but demonstrated God's abundant generosity to reach out to people of whatever sort who were in need. The parable of the wedding feast exemplifies the extremes to which God was prepared to go:

> The kingdom of heaven may be compared to a king who gave a marriage feast for his son, and sent his servants to call those who were invited to the marriage feast; but they would not come. Again he sent other servants, saying, 'Tell those who are invited, Behold, I have made ready my dinner, my oxen and my fat calves are killed, and everything is ready; come to the marriage feast.' But they made light of it and went off, one to his farm, another to his business, while the rest seized his servants, treated them shamefully, and killed them. The king was angry, and he sent his troops and destroyed those murderers and burned their city. Then he said to his servants, 'The wedding is ready, but those invited were not worthy. Go therefore to the thoroughfares, and invite to the marriage feast as many as you find.' And those servants went out into the streets and gathered all whom they found, both bad and good; so the wedding

hall was filled with guests. "But when the king came in to look at the guests, he saw there a man who had no wedding garment; and he said to him, 'Friend, how did you get in here without a wedding garment?' And he was speechless. Then the king said to the attendants, 'Bind him hand and foot, and cast him into the outer darkness; there men will weep and gnash their teeth.' For many are called, but few are chosen. [Mt 22.2-14]

The version given here is from St Matthew's Gospel, with quite a few of its details somewhat different from those found in St Luke's Gospel. The narrative is thereby more firmly contextualized in a Jewish setting; thus, the 'servants' mentioned are evidently the prophets of old, many of them disregarded or ill-treated, while the 'troops' are usually identified with those sent in by the occupying Roman force to sack Jerusalem in 70 AD in the wake of the Jewish revolt. Luke's second wave of invitations includes 'the poor, the maimed, the blind, the lame' – those who are too readily ignored in any society, the underprivileged who (so St Paul tells us) formed the bulk of the early Church; but in Matthew we read the startling words that the aim is more universal, as the king's servants gather 'all whom they found, both bad and good'. The most compelling illustration of this inclusiveness follows not much later in the story. At Jesus' 'last supper' with his disciples, even Judas Iscariot – into whom Satan has already entered [Lk 22.3] – joins fully in the meal, 'dipping his hand in the dish' [Mt 26.23] along with all the others, and with Jesus himself. Despite his evil intent Judas is not excluded, so great is the Lord's kindness.

In his gospel, therefore, Christ's reaches out to all; his mission is for the whole world, just as we pray in the Our Father ('thy kingdom come, on earth as it is in heaven'). Yet, if God's generosity knows no bounds, and his love seeks to exclude no-one, we may be too preoccupied with our own agenda to heed his invitation. 'The man who had no wedding garment' is typical of those who have forgotten whose banquet is being celebrated, who have in effect chosen to ignore their host. There are reminiscences here of St Paul's warning in his 1st letter to the Corinthians regarding the need for personal preparation before participating in the Church's eucharistic meal:

> Whoever, therefore, eats the bread or drinks the cup of the Lord in an unworthy manner will be guilty of profaning the body and blood of the Lord. Let a man examine himself, and so eat of the bread and drink of the cup. For anyone who eats and drinks without discerning the body eats and drinks judgment upon himself. That is why many of you are weak and ill, and some have died. But if we judged ourselves truly, we should not be judged. But when we are judged by the Lord, we are chastened so that we may not be condemned along with the world. [1 Cor 11.27-32]

Jesus' own counsel is of wider application: if, he indicates, God invites us to join him in the paradise that only he can provide (whether in heaven or on earth), then we are entering his very presence. This is where our human fulfilment lies and where our true joy is to be found; hence, if we are not spiritually 'clothed' for the occasion, we shall be unable to share its blessings. Elsewhere in the New Testament there are alternative descriptions of what is implied: 'Let us', says St Paul, 'put on the armour of light' [Rom 13.12] – and hopefully, the baptized have already 'put on Christ' [Gal 3.27]. His most detailed account is found in the passage quoted earlier from his letter to the Colossians, urging Christians to 'Put on ... compassion, kindness, lowliness, meekness, and patience' together with forbearance, mutual forgiveness, and 'above all ... love, which binds everything together in perfect harmony.' [Col 3.12-14]

St John the Divine too encourages the readers of his Apocalypse to 'perfect their works in the sight of God', with the promise that 'he who conquers shall be clad in white garments'. 'The fine linen', he says, 'is the righteous deeds of the saints' [Apoc 19.8], or again 'blessed are those who wash their robes' [Apoc 22.14] – they will enjoy 'the tree of life' i.e. gain the long dreamed-for paradise of God.

Interpreting the language

We may ask, however, is it consistent with the boundless mercy and generosity of God to be treated so harshly – bound 'hand and foot' and 'cast into the outer darkness' – if we fall woefully short of expectations? The language cannot of course be taken literally, but expresses in graphic imagery what it might mean to have effectively sidelined God from our lives, and to have rejected his guidance and his grace. When Jesus addressed his contemporaries, he spoke (as far as we know) mainly in their Aramaic tongue and used familiar idioms. It was still a Semitic culture (the term is derived from Shem, one of the sons of Noah) which retained features of a once harsh nomadic lifestyle, and a corresponding tendency to highlight the stark polarities of the desert. Speech might therefore have often been more graphic than today's modes of expression. Yet, despite – to our ears – his brutally vivid description of 'hell' (and the distinct possibility that the evangelist himself may have considerably elaborated Jesus' own words, bearing in mind that Luke concludes his version of the parable much more briefly), the point our Lord was making remains valid: if we choose to pursue our own goals instead of following the way of life that God revealed to us through him, the outcome will be darkness and disappointment, however it is imagined. It is not punishment inflicted upon us, but the inevitable consequence of false hopes and preferences. It may in reality mean, not so much 'hell' as frequently portrayed in lurid and terrifying detail, but simply *oblivion*.

The language and imagery of the New Testament has not always been appreciated adequately in the history of the Church. Despite its prevailing emphasis upon love as 'the fulfilling of the law' [Rom 13.10 cf. Mt 22.36-40], the temptation has sometimes been to isolate specific verses from their context and then treat them as legal imperatives. During my years teaching in Malawi at an ecumenical theological college, whenever one of our Calvinist students preached, he seemed able to extract a harsh injunction from almost any scripture so as to reinforce his key message, 'Obey God or he will punish you'. The Christian way of life was thus reduced to a codified morality, fostering fear and guilt in equal proportions.

When Jesus spoke, however, people were 'astonished' because he taught 'not as the scribes' [Mk 1.22] nor as some of the more prominent Pharisees. Unlike their stark polarity of 'black or white', his was the 'greyscale' approach of a storyteller whose characters are typically more complex creatures. Nor, for Jesus, was it a straightforward matter of observing a code of conduct; he invited deeper reflection:

> You have heard it said ... but I say to you ... unless your righteousness exceeds that of the scribes and Pharisees, you will never enter the

> kingdom of heaven ... you therefore must be perfect, as your heavenly Father is perfect. [Mt 5.21-48]

Jesus' aim was to inspire a new vision of God's purposes for mankind, and the way to human fulfilment:

> I came that they may have life, and have it abundantly. [Jn 10.10]

It was the dawn of a new era, grounded in God's own spiritual revelation. A temporal analogy might be the transition to a new regime of governance following a political and cultural revolution; although responsibilities, relationships and indeed laws might change, what would matter most would be the transformation in values and attitudes, as in people's aims and aspirations. I am reminded of challenging words from a poster that appeared in many Zimbabwe offices soon after the country's independence in 1980:

> *The Boss drives his men,*
> *The Leader inspires them.*
> *The Boss depends on authority,*
> *The Leader depends on goodwill.*
> *The Boss evokes fear,*
> *The Leader radiates love.*
> *The Boss says 'I',*
> *The Leader says 'We'.*
> *The Boss shows who is wrong,*
> *The Leader shows what is wrong.*
> *The Boss demands respect,*
> *The Leader commands respect.*
> *So be a leader, not a boss.*

The poster was alas! largely ineffective, and its analogy with Jesus' revolutionary image of his heavenly Father is far from perfect; but it does prompt us to remember that what underlies his teaching and practice is his uniquely authentic testimony to God's character:

> I do as the Father has commanded me. [Jn 14.31]

> This is eternal life, that they may know thee the only true God, and Jesus Christ whom thou hast sent. [Jn 17.3]

Throughout the scriptures references to the divine being have of course made use of human images and analogies – we have no other means of expressing ourselves, unless we extend 'language' beyond words into the realm of art or music. God has thus been termed 'king' or 'judge', but also 'shepherd' or 'father'. Such language is certainly valuable, provided its limitations are recognized: however, God is envisaged, his being is ultimately a mystery that cannot be simplified or condensed into human categories. Yet – and this was very evident to Marcion in the mid-2nd century – the temptation has often been to inject too much of our own way of thinking into our expectations of God, in effect exalting some particular way of portraying the divine above all the others. Marcion made the mistake of concluding that the Israelites of old, who (as in the book of Judges) once depicted God as a ruthless tyrant bent on genocide, therefore worshipped a different God from the Father of our Lord Jesus Christ, and so came to regard the Old Testament as unfit for Christian purposes. He was fortunately overruled, or we should have lost many profound insights found in other passages. Biblical scholars such as Origen were in any case insistent that the key to reading the Hebrew scriptures correctly was actually Christ himself: 'warfare', for example, is still necessary but as a spiritual, often internal, battle; or, to quote Pope Francis, that the deeper meaning of 'exodus' is as 'a constant pilgrimage across the various deserts of life'. Words and phrases may indeed hold layers of truth, ranging from the literal or the moral to the more profoundly spiritual.

It is nevertheless a perennial habit of religious people sometimes to prefer one particular mode of interpretation, regardless even of well-established alternatives. Literalism and fundamentalism continue to flourish both in Muslim and in Christian circles, promoting distorted readings of their respective scriptures. The resulting image of God then portrays a ruthless despot, as inflexible in his demands as his hard-line 'disciples'. Evidently there were certain Pharisees in Jesus' day who had succumbed to such authoritarianism, having lost sight of the strongly compassionate roots of their own history:

> When Israel was a child, I loved him, and out of Egypt I called my son.
> [Hos 11.1]

> How can I give you up, O Ephraim! How can I hand you over, O Israel! How can I treat you like Admah! How can I treat you like Zeboiim! My heart recoils within me, my compassion grows warm and tender. I will not execute my fierce anger, I will not again destroy Ephraim; *for I am God and not man, the Holy One in your midst, and I will not come to destroy.* [Hos 11.8-9]
>
> I will heal their faithlessness; I will love them freely, for my anger has turned from them. [Hos 14.4]

Jesus, the incarnate Son of God, restores the message of God's love and mercy, still extended to the 'children' he has created. He is not born in a palace but in a stable. He is a refugee at a young age. He devotes himself in adult life to helping and healing those in need. He offers his life for the salvation of us all. We have noted the terminology found in St John's Gospel, where Jesus describes himself as the Good Shepherd; he is also the Way, the Truth and the Life; he is the Resurrection and the Life; and when he thus speaks in these words he is surely echoing God's self-revelation to Moses at the burning bush:

> God said to Moses, "I am who I am." And he said, "Say this to the people of Israel, 'I am has sent me to you.'" [Exod 3.14]

If, therefore, we hope to find the fulness of life ourselves as God's children, made in his image, it is to Jesus that we must turn. The challenge for Christians – and expressed here once again in words of Pope Francis taken from *Evangelii Gaudium* ('the Joy of the Gospel') - is that we must 'go forth from our own comfort zone in order to reach all the peripheries in need of the light of the Gospel'; alternatively, in a recent message for World Mission Day, he describes the Church as 'a field hospital' into which we welcome the sick, the wounded, and the struggling:

> Mission reminds the Church that she is not an end unto herself, but a humble instrument and mediation of the Kingdom. A self-referential Church, one content with earthly success, is not the Church of Christ, his crucified and glorious Body. That is why we should prefer 'a Church which is bruised, hurting and dirty because it has been out on the streets, rather than a Church which is unhealthy from being confined and from clinging to its own security'.

Perhaps one day we shall be able to remind ourselves of this fundamental perspective by reciting a creed that not only confesses our faith, but mentions specifically God's mercy and the outreach of his love: we need to recall not only *who* Jesus is, but *why* he came among us.

> *Lord God,*
> *Give to us the readiness to seek truth without fear.*
> *When we are perplexed, teach us to be patient.*
> *When we encounter doubt, help us to persevere.*
> *When illumination comes, keep us humble,*
> *Knowing that you are beyond our knowledge.*
> *Enrich our thoughts with your wisdom,*
> *And kindle our hearts with your love,*
> *That we may press forward to see you face to face.*
> *In Jesus' name we pray.*

As we walk in the steps of our Lord, we recognise our daily need to commune (as he did) with 'Our Father who art in heaven', to struggle (as he did) against temptation, to find counsel (as he did) in our holy scriptures, to listen (as he did) to the cries of those in pain around us, to persevere (as he did) even when suffering ourselves, and to forgive (as he did) those who do us harm. It is such personal witness to his Gospel values that will eventually bear fruit, both for others and for ourselves. Our goal is, with the help and guidance of the Holy Spirit, to align ourselves completely with God's purposes, so that his kingdom comes and his will is done.

www.ingramcontent.com/pod-product-compliance
Lightning Source LLC
Chambersburg PA
CBHW051543230426
43669CB00015B/2712